One American Boy

One American Boy

◆

The Dolph Crawford Story

Dolph Crawford, with Rusty Fischer

iUniverse, Inc.

New York Lincoln Shanghai

One American Boy
The Dolph Crawford Story

iUniverse, Inc.

For information address:
iUniverse, Inc.
2021 Pine Lake Road, Suite 100
Lincoln, NE 68512
www.iuniverse.com

Note: This is a work of nonfiction. The events, characters, and events happened, as reported, during my time before, during, and after I was "One American Boy," and are based on personal knowledge, interviews, recollections, and newspaper articles. Names and addresses with an asterisk (*) have been changed to protect the innocent.

ISBN: 0-595-32079-1 (pbk)
ISBN: 0-595-66475-X (cloth)

Printed in the United States of America

To my Mom and Dad: I appreciate all your love and support over the years. I know that I kept a lot of secrets from you. I didn't really allow you to know me. But please understand that I was trying to know myself. I hope when you read this book you will understand me better. My life has always been complex, but that was mostly because I wasn't being true to myself. I now love and respect myself and finally have the courage to be honest about who I am to myself and the world.

Mom: You taught me love and compassion. Thank you for always listening and making me feel loved.

Dad: Thanks for teaching me how to be tough in life. You knew my life would be very difficult and you knew that I would encounter people who would want to hurt me. I believe you did your best. I may not have been the son you wanted. But I hope you know that I love you.

Charlie: Thanks for being the son that Dad always wanted. Thanks for giving him grandchildren and great grandchildren. Thanks for being the "good son" that any father would be proud of. Thank you, I suppose, for being the son that *I* couldn't be.

Gaye: Thanks for teaching me how to shave (my face). It's funny now I shave my legs and my chest, too. I tell people jokingly that it's because I learned how to shave from a girl.

Dana: My heart. You have always been the one who showed me so much love and kindness and support. Thank you for the countless hours of telephone conversations where you listened and didn't judge. Thanks for encouraging me in anything that I set out to do. Thanks for making me understand that not all heterosexual men are monsters. You have a great man in your husband, Mike. You were the first person in my family that I told I was gay. You always tried to protect me from the "wolves" in the world that tried to devour me. You are a true angel from heaven. I love you more than words can say.

Scoop: My childhood friend. Since kindergarten we were inseparable. We laughed our way through some tough years in Bridge City. We have been close and distant through our adult years, but at times I think life took us in different directions. Scoop, I think of you often and all our childhood times and I smile. God Bless you.

David: My mentor. You brought me "out" in such style. You supported me. You helped me get my first credit card. I remember the kindest thing you ever did for me: one summer when I was going to move to a new apartment you drove five hours to Dallas and called me from a corner payphone and surprised me. You helped me move and get set up in my new home. I really needed you at that point in my life. I have kept every one of your cards and letters you sent me through the years at different stages in our lives. I love one of your disco quotes:

> *"You gotta keep dancin'*
> *Smilin'*
> *To keep from breakin' apart..."*

I am still dancin', David...I hope you are, too.

My dear Francesca: You are my "bridge over troubled water." You came into my life through some of my worst years. You stood by me and weathered the storm with me, when others chose to jump ship. You have been my rock. You understand me. I feel that. I love you and your kids, Maia and Florina. I hope that all three of you are forever a part of my life.

My friend, John: Sugar, you have always said that it's "all about you." Well, you say that, but you have been a good friend to me. You couldn't come in the court room but you stood outside and gave your support. Looking back, I guess that's how you've always been in our friendship: Watching from a distance. Thank you for helping me in tough financial times. Thanks for hanging with me through some very turbulent legal times, as well. Although you try to seem superficial, I feel you care and I have witnessed your unselfish love. Maybe it's not all "about you," after all. I think that's your shield to keep from getting hurt. I will never hurt you. Always know I love you.

For those who were a part of my life and are now with God in Heaven, watching my final journey:

Grandma Effie: You were a character; you taught not to take things too seriously. You taught me it was okay to make fun of myself.

Aunt Dale: I saw cancer destroy your body, but it never destroyed your soul or your spirit. You were a loving and caring aunt. I know you are in a better place. Your spirit is free.

Phil Copeland: You gave me my first job. You encouraged me to be successful. You loved me and I felt that. You and your wife were so special to me. I miss you both.

Kevin: You brought me into a world that was exciting and scary at the same time. You were a great man. I believe you could have been very successful in any business. You kept your AIDS a secret. I wish you would have shared your secret with me. I could have understood you better.

I loved and admired you…

Ted: You were my friend. You built Trac Productions and made it successful. You were taken too soon. You were a great producer/director. I wish I could have done more for you. You taught me patience.

For all the young men and women who were taken too soon by AIDS: I still do not understand how this disease ever happened. It still doesn't make sense to me. I feel that so many of you were taken too young, before you had a chance to leave your mark on this world. You are with me as I write this book. You are with me when I speak to large audiences about being gay in America. You are with me when I get outraged about the slow process of politics and drug research. I hear you; I am trying to evoke change. You will leave your marks on this earth through me.

I will be your vessel.

I *am* listening…

Contents

Acknowledgements

Rusty Fischer: My "surprisingly heterosexual" writing partner. Thanks for believing in my story from the very beginning. You encouraged me to put it down on paper, when I wasn't even sure I wanted to re-live it in the first place. You helped me find a publisher. You advised me on contracts.

But most of all, you lent me your incredible gift as a writer and took my words and made them both powerful and strong. In the process, you shaped my story into a great book. I appreciate you more than you know. I cannot thank you enough for being the one single voice that will enable my words to be finally heard.

I consider you not just my co-author, but my *friend*…

I have acknowledged Hollywood and TV and the popular media for helping further the gay rights movement in the text of my book. Now I would like to single out some special people who, in my mind, helped me personally by their movies or television shows and by using their voice to make the world a better place for not only "Dolph Crawford," but for the millions of other gays and lesbians that I consider my brothers and sisters:

Cher: I have danced to many of her greatest hits over the last three decades. I finally had a chance to meet Cher in 1981. It was a time when I was coming into my own as a gay male. Coincidently, Cher was just coming into her own as an actress.

I met this daring diva in New York while she was starring in *Come Back to the Five and Dime: Jimmy Dean, Jimmy Dean*. I waited nervously backstage to meet a woman that I always felt connected to, ever since I had seen her and Sonny at the Houston Live stock show concert years before. I was standing there thinking back on all her great songs.

Suddenly, the backstage door opened and there she stood. She was so kind to me. We talked and she posed for a picture with me. Her last words to me before she got into her limo were, "You're cute, babe." I never forgot our encounter. I even included a picture of Cher and I in 1981 in the book. (As you can see, we have both changed a lot over the years.)

Phil Donahue: Through his talk show, Phil helped me understand that I was not alone. He taught me that AIDS was a true killer in *all* communities. He taught me that I could protect myself from getting HIV. Phil spoke about issues that were not yet acceptable in mainstream television.

Phil Donahue did an incredible job and evoked change early on about the gay movement, in general, and the AIDS crisis, in particular. Rather than merely basking in the limelight, Phil used his celebrity to open up a dialogue and begin to understand diversity in American culture at a time when America wasn't ready to hear such "immoral" context. Though he was later eclipsed by shock TV and tabloid journalism, he was a true pioneer.

Oprah Winfrey: Another pioneer, Oprah Winfrey taught me about using my life to change society while I was watching her talk show about her "Angel Network," where she introduced the idea of changing your community by volunteering your time or resources. I decided to volunteer at the AIDS resource center and give back to my community.

Later on, I decided to tell my story in this book to help young people or a gay person of any age who might be struggling with issues about his or her own sexuality and the repercussions of coming out to his family or friends. I guess I owe a big part of this book to Oprah. Girl, you have been my friend for eighteen years, even though we have never met. You have been a friend to America as well. "Run-on," O.W., I will continue to watch your journey.

Rosie O'Donnell: She doesn't get enough credit for being a leader in the gay community. Rosie has lent her celebrity to causes like gay adoption, and most recently gay marriage. She risked her well-known career and magazine and even crippling lawsuits for being true to who she is and what she stands for.

I have the utmost respect for Rosie because she took a chance with her entire career and stepped up for gay rights and children's rights and human rights across this country. I love you, Rosie, and I hope to meet you one day.

Ellen Degeneres: Thanks, Ellen, for "coming out" and risking everything to stay true to yourself. Although it appeared after you came out that your career faltered, you rallied like always, Ellen, and now have an incredible talk show: *The Ellen Show*. You bring humor and kindness to your one-hour show every day. You continue to make me laugh. "Keep on swimming," Ellen. I have great respect for you.

Joan Rivers: Joni, you were one of the first celebrities to be an AIDS activist. I remember seeing you in gay bars in California in the 80s doing fund raisers. You were active at a time when no other celebrities were. You have never taken credit for that. You were also the first comedienne my Mom saw live in Las Vegas in the early 80s. My Mom couldn't stop laughing at your comedy routine. Thanks for making us all laugh over the years, Joni.

Rock Hudson: For finally going public about his disease. Most celebrities of his caliber would have died quietly and listed cause of death as "cancer." Rock chose to leave this earth as he had entered it…a legend.

Dame Elizabeth Taylor: For your never ending fight for AIDS research. You worked diligently with AMFAR and have helped raise millions of dollars and even lobbied Congress. You made America, and the world, aware and perhaps more educated about this horrible disease than anyone. Liz, you proved you are truly a "Grand Dame."

Sir Elton John: You were one of the first stars to use your celebrity for raising money for AIDS research. You started a foundation and raised millions for the cause. You also took a chance in "coming out" and portraying an incredible relationship with your lover, David. Elton, you will not only be remembered as an incredible singer and performer, you will also leave a legacy of being a humble humanitarian.

Bob Paris: You were an incredible bodybuilder in the 90s. You were destined to be the next Mr. Olympia. I believe you could have been the next Arnold Schwarzenegger. You risked it all and came out publicly about your homosexuality on the cover of a muscle magazine. Bob, you were the first homosexual male that I looked at as a role model. I respect you for your honesty. I have read all your books and look forward to seeing more of you in the future.

About this Book

When I was born on May 26, 1963 I had already broken a law: Homosexuality was illegal in Texas. I grew up in a household with loving parents who gave their life to raising four children. I was the different one, the emotional one, the 'pretty boy' that didn't fish, hunt, play sports, or enjoy camping. "Sissy" was a word I heard most often.

"Fag" was another…

I grew up in a small town called Bridge City, Texas; population about 8,000 mostly white heterosexuals with pickup trucks in their driveways and confederate flags on their sagging porches.

Its motto was 'Friendly people on the Grow.' The most popular landmark was the Port Arthur Bridge, mostly because of the endless string of depressed people who jumped from it to their death.

I guess they weren't "growing" anymore…

Thus begins the scathing new memoir by former gay porn star Dolph Crawford, **One American Boy**: *The Dolph Crawford Story*. Video pornography has been a staple of gay male culture for decades—according to *Adult Video News*, the industry churns out 11,000 titles each year, more than 20 times as many as Hollywood—but there is little written about the people who perform or produce this entertainment.

Until now, that is…

Endowed with that "pretty boy" face—and a body to match—Dolph Crawford used both to wrangle his way to fortune and fame. At his peak, Dolph was one of the undisputed kings of gay porn.

But along the way his life was filled with the inevitable ups and downs of a young gay boy growing up in mostly heterosexual Texas. Alienation, shame, guilt, and self-hatred were the substance of his youth, and when he left home in his teens he didn't fare much better.

Fueled by confusion and pain, he entered the alluring but toxic world of male hustling, dancing, and eventually signed with adult video powerhouse Vivid Entertainment to not only act in but also produce and direct some of the company's most popular gay porn videos, many of which are still considered "classics" to this day, thus fueling Dolph's enduring stature as he tours convention centers and signs autographs throughout the country.

Says the author, "There are many stereotypes in this country, which makes it easier for people to be put in a certain box and labeled. I could be put in several boxes: porn star, hustler, fag, or felon.

"The only stereotype that I accept is *One American Boy*.

"I write about the experience of growing up gay in America and dealing with day-to-day life. Although my experiences are a bit more dramatic than most people's are, they were all stepping stones. I made many mistakes in my life, most of which are documented on my 'permanent record.' But I came through it and turned it around and lived to tell about it.

"Life is hard for most people, but life for a homosexual in a heterosexual world can be overwhelmingly more difficult. We are on the brink of change in the United States, politically speaking.

"For the first time in our history, gay rights will be a political issue that could make or break a presidential candidate. I want to be a voice for the gay community. I want to help the next generation of young people be able to make informed decisions about the choices they make.

"I don't choose to preach, I choose to inform, the final decision that a person makes about his or her path in life is hopefully an informed one. I don't buy into the 'hype.' I now read between the lines and make an educated decision based on people I respect and opinions I value. It took a long time to get to that point. I hope this book speeds up the process for those who read it…"

Now Dolph bares all in a revealing memoir that rips the glamour off the video industry as effectively as it unearths the enduring pain of growing up gay in an America that, despite the recent groundswell of interest spurned on by shows like *Will & Grace* and *Queer Eye for the Straight Guy*, still forces its morals and disdain down the gay establishment's throat.

PROLOGUE:
Busted?

It was a few days before Christmas when the phone rang, interrupting a marathon wrapping session, not to mention Bing Crosby's *White Christmas*. I scampered across the living room floor of my apartment, dodging boxes, rolls of gaily patterned wrapping paper, scissors, and tape as I wrapped presents to take home with me to Bridge City, the town of my birth.

The voice on the other end of line was destined to be no grandmother wishing me "Happy Holidays," nor even the sound of my boyfriend, business partner, and mentor Kevin, who was sick and lying low this holiday.

In his stead, he had forwarded the many calls that normally went to his place to come to mine, and thus I was the head phone answerer, chef, and bottle washer answering the phones for what had grown to be a rather large escort service in the metro Dallas area.

Business was booming, thus the small stack of wrapped presents lying pitifully next to the towering mountain of as yet *unwrapped* presents. Needless to say, the sound of ringing phones, and even Bing Crosby, was slowly getting on my already frazzled nerves.

Still, we hadn't become the biggest male escort service in Dallas by letting our emotions get the better of us, and so I was exceedingly polite and businesslike as I answered the phone that cold December day.

It was a new client, calling from his room at the nearby Brookhollow Inn. My jive meter went off instantly; there was just something…*off*…about this particular caller. Answer the phones long enough, and you hear the same things every day. The same buzz words, requests, negotiations, appreciation, expectation. It's enough to school you in what sounds different.

This guy was *definitely* different…

His phrasing was all off; his timing, too. There was something hesitant in his voice, a nervousness that made him sound like the typical homophobic hetero male. Not that we didn't get our share of these "bi-curious" types, but this one sounded angrier than the normal husband stepping out on his wife. In the back of my head was a fateful caveat from Kevin, who had recently warned me that there were a lot of Dallas vice cracking down on male escort services in the area.

I am not sure if it was the underlying hatred of heterosexual males or just pure pride…but I put down my Christmas wrapping paper and took the call personally. Not one to be intimidated, I told the caller that I would be sending a model named "Dolph" to his room.

He agreed and the time was set up to meet at his hotel room. I finished wrapping my presents, showered, made myself presentable, and hit the road. The streets were jammed with last-minute shoppers, every radio station blared carols—more Bing Crosby—and blinking lights could be seen in every passing window, but I felt anything but seasonal cheer.

My boyfriend was "sick," the AIDS crisis was in full bloom, the Dallas vice squad was everywhere, and now I could be showing up to a trap without even wanting to taste the cheese. Bah humbug…

The appointment was booked for 7 p.m., but I showed up early.

I located the appointed room and listened outside the door, staring down at well-trod carpet and hoping the inhabitants inside couldn't hear my heart pounding through my chest on the other side of the door.

Then again, it would have been hard for them to: I heard many voices inside the room and a porno on Spectra-vision was blaring on the TV. (I assumed, rightfully so, that the taxpayers of Dallas were paying for that little holiday perk.)

Pride, anger, betrayal, and even curiosity forced my only slightly trembling hand to the door as I knocked, forcefully. Everyone inside the room got real quiet, real fast. Finally, a fat bald man opened the door and looked at me with equal parts curiosity and contempt. It was a particularly coy sneer I'd seen once too often in my life, but now it was too late.

I was here.

He was here.

Our destinies were now intertwined…

He was wearing more polyester than a prom king, but looked more appropriate for the part of the aging principal than the vital jock. I noticed a smattering of perspiration dotting his broad, red forehead and smelled the waft of cheap cologne emanating from his coarse, open pores. I introduced myself as Dolph and extended my hand, expecting a firm handshake. What I got was a very insecure, obviously undercover officer telling me to "come inside."

I entered and told him I had to "check in" with the escort service. In reality, I simply called my apartment and talked to the answering machine while I pretended I was talking to a live person. At this point, however, no one even knew where I was. Kevin was too ill to run things personally, and with the holidays upon us we were more short-staffed than usual.

Talk about flying solo…

I was doing this by myself…*for* myself. I was finally facing "the enemy." The undercover officer immediately started trying to get me to agree to sexual favors for money and, when I told him that was not what I did, he became very agitated. His flop sweat multiplied, his cheap cologne turned rancid, and his mood grew equal parts superior and sour.

He looked far too old to be a rookie, but his bad acting made me wonder if this was his first day going undercover. He paced in tight circles on the cheap carpet, running a big, beefy hand through his non-existent hair and straining the seams of his polyester pants as he strode past two double-beds with gaudy comforters.

Around this time in Dallas a few cops had been injured in the line of duty, and because I came early they didn't have all the surveillance equipment set up, so the officers in the adjoining rooms could not hear the exchange between the homophobic officer and me.

Far be it from me to give them the time to do so now…

I rushed on, and shortly was in the middle of explaining to him that I was what was known as a "paid companion" and that there was "no sex involved." I quoted him the statue under state law, by memory, a skill that, in addition to fellatio and proper restaurant etiquette, was mandatory for anyone who worked for Kevin, that defines "…money exchanged for sexual favors is considered prostitution and that was a misdemeanor in the state of Texas."

But before I could finish my eloquent speech, six officers burst in the room with their guns drawn and eyes loaded with fear and self-loathing. I was scared. Probably the most scared I'd been during my few short years as a male escort.

It's a fear few heterosexuals know: There I was at the mercy of seven homophobic, good-ole-boy, pot bellied, donut eating cops with guns pointed and eyes blazing.

The officer that was pretending—and poorly at that—to be a "client" was pissed off because the other officers had just blown his cover. (I wanted to tell him he'd been doing a fine job of that all by his lonesome, but didn't want to spoil the moment as the color of his jowly face turned an ever brighter shade of red.)

He then identified himself as Dallas vice and I was told that the escort service was "being investigated for prostitution." I listened quietly until I had finally inched past the cops with guns and then I simply explained that the service I worked for did not promote prostitution, simply companionship.

Although my "client" argued that there was no such thing, it was obvious to one and all that nothing illegal had transpired that night and, eager to leave before they made something up, I quickly made my exit.

I was shaken.

I had come face to face with the enemy and walked away, unscathed.

This time…

But what about next time? As I drove home to finish up wrapping my Christmas presents, hands as white as snow on the steering wheel, I knew that my days were numbered.

I hadn't been unreasonable to think that I could have been killed in that situation. Many were the popular urban legends of the era that told of gay escorts showing up for a trick and never…*ever*…coming back.

Had I narrowly avoided being one of them? The scare left me shaken, bereft, and ungrounded. I drove home on auto-pilot, steering through town as the blinking Christmas lights faded in and out of my rearview mirror.

They say in the face of death your life flashes before your eyes. Well, I'd always been a slow learner. It wasn't until after I left those vice cops far, far behind that I began reflecting on the life that had brought us all to that violent intersection so close to Christmas. Amazingly, I had the Dallas PD to thank for introducing me to the Ghost of Christmas Past…

1

Friendly People on the Grow

Growing up gay in the 1970's wasn't easy. But if you lived in the south, it was even more difficult. I was born on May 26, 1963 and at that time there were actually laws on the books against homosexuality in Texas.

Think about it: I had just entered the world and already I had broken the law. It seemed a bad omen and, unfortunately, it would not be the last time I would have a brush with violating that particular Texas Statute.

Turns out I would be the last of four children. My father wanted a son, though he already had my brother, Charlie, who was the oldest of our brood. However, Charlie was my mother's son from a previous marriage and, in my Dad's eyes, that just "didn't count."

I'm sure my father was thrilled when I finally came into this world. If Charlie was his son in spirit, I then was to be his son in legacy. The name, the genes, the flesh, the blood.

My Dad couldn't have been prouder.

At least for a little while…

Nonetheless, Charlie was the "Golden Boy" of my family and always would be. But then, how could my poor Dad resist a kid like Charlie? After all, he excelled in all sports, he was popular, he was smart, and everyone in town knew who he was. Actually, Charlie was more like my father than I—his firstborn son—would ever be.

My Dad and Charlie were very close. I am glad my Mom had Charlie; he would be the son that my father never had in me. But in true heterosexual fashion I think my Dad wanted someone to carry on his name, his legacy, since Charlie's last name was different from his own.

Ever the dutiful wife, Mom quickly got pregnant again. This time Dana, my sister, was born. Dana was destined be a quiet, loving person. Unlike her big brother, Charlie, she never wanted the spotlight, and was always interested in pleasing her parents. She worked in the yard with my Dad, she helped my Mom around the house. Although she was just an average student, she had an incredible heart.

Over the years, Dana would become my best friend, my heart, my second Mom. She is still very special to me in my life today. But no matter how hard she tried, she wasn't the boy my Dad desperately wanted.

So two years later Mom was pregnant again, this time dishing up Dad's second disappointment: another girl, this time named Gaye. Interesting name; Mom thought that Gaye meant happy, joyous, carefree.

At least, that's how my Mom viewed that name back in 1961.

Now, of course, it means something entirely different…

She obviously didn't know any gay people. And how could she? After all, according to my parents, homosexuals just "didn't exist in this small Texas town." (Little did she know they existed a lot closer than she thought!)

For her part, my future sister Gaye was a vibrant redhead with a splash of freckles thrown in for good measure. Though no Charlie, she was nonetheless the "tom boy" of the two girls, the one who loved to play sports, build tree forts, and be carefree.

Unlike Dana, who preferred to stand in the shadows, Gaye *loved* to be the center of attention. She would be the person to teach me how to shave (my face). She would also be the first person on earth to call me a "fag."

She is now a mother of three; she grew out of her tom boy stage and, secretly, I think she wishes that her little brother *wasn't* a "fag." But, once again, with no boy to call his own, my father desperately wanted to try again.

The doctors told my mother that it would be difficult to have another child at her age, but my Mom, always trying to please, nonetheless tried once more. And, in 1963, unto my Dad a boy child was finally born.

Even from the very beginning, I was the pretty boy, the quiet boy, the sensitive one, the boy that didn't like to fish, hunt, or play sports, the boy that was the diametric opposite of the son my father had always dreamed of.

Still they named me "Johnny Wayne," after the *True Grit* star and legendary man's man, that old salt John Wayne. My father was ecstatic, passing out cigars to all his cronies and boasting of all the football records, home runs, and broken hearts to come. (Well, at least 1 out of 3 ain't bad.)

Johnny Wayne, his son, was the apple of his eye. Well, as the mystery of the universe would have it, I was not exactly the boy that my Dad dreamed of. My Dad and Charlie would always take me fishing and hunting, trying their damndest to indoctrinate me in all things hetero; I hated it.

I remember one time being in a duck blind smack dab in the middle of hunting season. For those of you unfamiliar with such modern forms of southern torture, the duck blind is a place were heterosexual men hang out at 4:30 a.m. in a desolate marsh, waiting for innocent ducks to land so they can blow them out of the water with shotgun shells "for sport."

I clearly remember sitting in this blind with these two hetero-men, listening to them talking about pussy and drinking and laughing and realizing that I must be some kind of alien, because I couldn't relate to any of it.

Not a single word.

Finally, the moment they had been waiting for arrived: the ducks began to emerge, landing beautifully in the placid pond that was their home. Such a stunning sight, seeing the beauty of nature and being a part of the majesty surrounding such striking creatures. But then I noticed the other men in the duck blind—my Dad and my brother, no less—getting their guns out and adjusting their firing positions to kill these beautiful birds!

I don't know what came over me, but I immediately began yelling and shooing the ducks away in hopes that they would fly to safety! Once I was sure they were safe, I turned around to some very angry hetero-men sitting tensely in the duck blind. Men who were no longer talking about pussy; now they were calling *me* a pussy.

Needless to say, I was never invited to go hunting again. My Mom tried to explain to me that men are just "born hunters," that was just "bred into" men, to hunt. I remember thinking at the time, "I am a man and I don't want to kill or injure animals, it's senseless. I admire nature for its beauty, and I would never upset that delicate balance just to fill a few empty hours on a weekend morning."

What *was* innate in me was the inherent belief that killing something for sport is senseless. I would later learn, of course, that Texas made a big sport out of killing. The death penalty, after all, is alive and well in Texas. Still today, one of the biggest killing machines is that on Texas' death row. And in Texas there is very rarely a pardon from the governor.

Such is the bloodlust of my home state.

But there I was, dropped into this small town in Texas called "Bridge City." Population? About 8,000 at that time. The motto on the billboard as you drove into town read "Bridge City Texas: The Home of Friendly People on The Grow."

The idea behind the city's name was that you couldn't really get to the small town without crossing a bridge. One such bridge that you had to cross was The

Port Arthur Bridge, also called the "rainbow bridge" because it was high and round, sort of resembling a rainbow.

I always found this to be ironic because the gay emblem, symbolizing love, peace, and universal acceptance would eventually become the "Rainbow," also representing diversity. But the people in Bridge City didn't know that when they referred to the Rainbow Bridge.

This bridge was the main entrance—and exit—into my small hometown. To a young gay man growing up in the 60s and 70s, it might as well have been a drawbridge and a moat.

At the time it was narrow and had one lane going in either direction. With no shoulder. Many people who were depressed or angry or maybe just...*different*...jumped to their death from that bridge.

I guess they weren't "Growing" anymore...

I would cross that bridge many times in my life, coming and going from my small town. As I would inevitably reach the top and look down into that deep swirl of water, I would often think of those poor souls who had jumped to their death. I would wonder if they found peace, at last. I would mourn for them, but quietly I would mourn even more deeply for myself.

After all, they had jumped, they had taken the plunge, they were gone now. At peace, free from the slings and arrows of schoolmates and siblings and even parents. I was left here, alone, in a world that I was beginning to understand that I didn't really fit into.

A world where if you were different from the norm you were locked away, you were called crazy, and you were feverishly whispered about on the back porches amongst the family members that had the gossip on everyone—and everything—in my small town. The same back porches that proudly displayed the confederate flag.

Bridge City wasn't far from Vidor, Texas, where the KKK was alive and well. Every so often, there were rallies held in my small town. It was never questioned. There wasn't one black person in Bridge City, not one, and not for the entire eighteen years I lived there, not in schools, church, the grocery store, or the local library.

I remember one time when I picked up a coin from the street I was told to put that down because: "...it was dirty, a nigger could have held that same coin!" I never understood hate, I never understood prejudice, but I knew that people in my small town used their white bed sheets for something other than sleeping on, and that was ever present in Bridge City.

I just assumed at the time it was all part of being "Friendly People on the Grow."

The biggest problem for me was that, in addition to blacks, Jews, Catholics, feminists, and just about everybody else who wasn't a white Protestant male of European-American descent, the KKK didn't like homosexuals, either.

Deep down inside I knew that to avoid the inherent danger of all those not so secret Klan members I would have to keep my sexual identity a secret until I got over that Rainbow Bridge and far, far away from my small town.

To where I didn't quite know at the moment, but I knew there *must* be someplace where there were people like me. Quiet, giving, loving people who didn't leave perfectly good coins on the ground because a black person had touched them or shoot ducks "for sport."

For now, though, I was stuck in Bridge City...

Like most kids I grew up in a loving household, with both a mother and a father. My Dad worked very hard at the local refinery and put in a lot of overtime to support a family of six.

My mother was a wonderful Mom. She kept a perfect house, and cooked and listened endlessly to each one of her children. Today, she is partially deaf in one ear, and I often wonder if we didn't talk her ear off.

Literally...

She treated each one of us with love, compassion, and care. I loved to make her laugh; she had, and still has, the greatest laugh I've ever heard. Looking back, I think I sensed some sadness within my Mom, so I felt that if I kept her laughing she wouldn't be so sad anymore. I wouldn't truly realize what great parents I had until I was much older. I now know that I was very lucky.

Like most parents, my Mom and Dad were not equipped to raise a homosexual son. After all, that just didn't happen in Bridge City, where people were too busy "growing" a bumper crop of card-carrying heterosexuals.

This is just one of the many reasons I decided to write this book. I think it is finally time that parents have something to read if they think there child is gay, or even just "different."

I believe every child is different, special, and unique. We live in a society where there are too many conformists. No one dares to be different. At forty years old, it is my belief that we all have a gift to share in this life. We bring something to this earth, no matter what it may be, and if we share that gift with the world we somehow leave this earth a better place than how we found it.

If you love yourself and are comfortable with who you are and you realize your reason for being on this earth, then somehow you don't judge or hate or try to destroy the beauty that is called life.

My advice to parents of gay children is simple: Let your child understand it first, before you confront him or her with it. Even though it may be something you suspect as a mother or a father, your child may still be struggling with it.

Homosexuality was never something I struggled with.

There was no doubting whether I was or I wasn't. I was only struggling with what I had been socialized to believe: that "…being homosexual was wrong, sick, a crime against nature, a sin against God." I heard it in church, in school, amongst friends, and within my own family.

I was struggling to keep a secret, to figure things out on my terms and in my own way. I went through the same obstacles that all kids go through, being liked by my peers, fitting in, growing as a person, coming into my own as a man, understanding my life's "calling."

There are parents who are totally against homosexuality, either for personal or religious beliefs. I must address those parents by saying that the universe has a funny way of educating you, because chances are there is a person close to you that *is* homosexual that you are hurting with your words right now.

Chances are there is a child or a brother or a sister who is struggling with telling you or revealing themselves completely to you because they don't want to be rejected or unloved.

You see, folks, that's all we want in life as humans—to love and be loved. As babies we want to be held and cuddled and kissed and loved. As adults we want love and intimacy and passion. When we lay dying we want someone to be there to hold our hands and put their arms around us and hold us.

Love is a universal need. Sex is simply a power that is extremely strong, that very few people—gay or straight—have learned how to control or conquer. But love is something that we all desire.

Unconditional love means that you love your brother or sister or mother or father or child *no matter what*. Whether they are gay or straight, Christian, Jew, black, white or Muslim, sitting in the front row of church or on death row in Texas, someone loves them…at least, I hope.

My struggle back then was to keep my secret, and to push anyone away who tried to get too close and figure me out. I pushed my parents away, my friends, my coworkers. I was a great actor; I never truly revealed my true self, until I finally lost sight of who I was, that is

By then it was almost too late to get myself back.…

When I speak to parents these days I don't preach. I talk about my experience and try to give insight on what their child might be going through. I also don't believe parents should try "outing" there child, either.

Let that child understand who he or she is, first. Give your kids some space. A parent's job is to let their kids know they are loved. They are safe and they are not judged. That is the best gift we can give our children.

A parent should promote individuality, model acceptance, and most of all *listen*. Let the child speak, let the child form opinions of his or her own. Children want their parent's approval; they will hide something that they feel a parent does not agree with. If you truly listen to your child and read between the lines, you will begin to understand your child and what his or her gifts are.

As I write this book it is an election year in the United States. I just read an interview about Vice President Dick Cheney, another good ole Texas boy. In the interview he speaks about how gays have "no right to be married," have no right to a "legal union." He agrees with President Bush on defining what marriage is in the constitution, "Between a man and a woman."

In the meantime, in his personal life, his daughter has admitted that she is homosexual. I often wonder how much he loves his own daughter. Because what he is doing in his political life is hurting his child in her personal life.

He is not validating who she is. He is not trying to use his power to make his daughter's life any easier. He is disrespecting his own flesh and blood by pandering to the religious right.

When he draws his last breath on earth, none of the members of the special interest groups he is courting today will be at his bedside, none of the conservative Republicans that give to his campaign now will comfort him in his final hours then.

Chances are his daughter will be there, however, holding him, comforting him. Chances are the last thing he sees will be her face, her sad eyes, and then and only then will he get it, only then will he see clearly what a gift he brought into this world in this child, how he could have changed the course of history out of respect for his own daughter. But by that time it will simply be too late.

That, I feel, will be his biggest regret…

The oil from Haliburton via Iraq will not comfort him, the millions from PAC money will not soothe his pain, but his daughter will put her arms around him and hold him and comfort him, even though he didn't comfort her when he could have. When he should have.

No matter who, or more importantly *what*, she was…

As gay people we are compassionate and caring, we root for the underdog, we love unconditionally. We understand heterosexuals better than they understand homosexuals. (Chances are, we understand heterosexuals better than they understand themselves!) We feel, we understand pain and suffering, we are moral and we are clear about who we are, because inevitably we have already given up a lot to be true to who we are.

Sometimes it takes us years to understand what our gift to this earth is supposed to be. I never dreamed I would someday write a book, and I certainly never thought I would tell my personal story, warts and all.

But the universe, apparently, had other plans.

You see, on November 19, 1999 my rights were taken away from me by the "Great State of Texas." I cannot tell you about that particular part of my life because the State of Texas has forbidden that I speak about it. If I do, they say, I will go to prison for a *very* long time.

It is the year 2004 when I write this book, and I still cannot speak of "that year." I am still under a gag order by the great state of Texas, because there are rich conservative Texans that are well-known in Dallas that never want me to speak or tell the truth.

I have exhausted all my money on attorneys, some of which were good ole boys that weren't very ethical in representing my best interests, either because they were homophobic or had a political or financial interest in seeing the other side emerge victorious. I lost my right to justice, to speak or write about the case—or the year, for that matter—of 1999.

We take rights for granted in this country. Of course, I never knew what I had until mine were gone. "Freedom of Speech" is very important, now more than ever. It seems as if this country has grown afraid, much like during the McCarthy era when Americans feared being black-listed or incarcerated for their beliefs.

It seems if you speak out against the war in Iraq you are accused of being anti-American. I feel I have very few rights left. I cannot marry another man. I cannot benefit from the same rights that any other married couple has. I cannot adopt, I cannot vote, I cannot sit on a jury and now I cannot write or draw or speak about what happened in Texas on November 19, 1999.

Or, more importantly, what happened afterward...

I believe that the universe's plan was for me to tell my story to those who are like me; to help my fellow human who may be lost or hurting or feeling alone. So with the help and encouragement of a professional author (who surprisingly is *heterosexual*) I begin my story. I hope that you understand my journey, and perhaps become enlightened along the winding path we are both about to start upon together.

I hope it speaks to you and you get something from it. It has been a crazy journey in the last forty years. Many ups and downs, a lot of drama, a lot of pain, lost loves, lost lives, and through it all I persevered.

I have been called many things in my life: "fag, sissy, hustler, porn star, criminal, and felon." I don't relate to any of that. I simply see myself as *One American Boy*. I hope you enjoy my journey. But most importantly, I hope that my story opens up a frank and encouraging dialogue about gay rights in America and, perhaps, human rights around the world.

2

Elvis Has Left the Building

I am often asked when I knew for sure that I was gay. The answer is very vivid to me: It was 1971 at the Houston Astrodome Livestock Rodeo. My parents took all of us kids there for a mini-vacation that year.

The rodeo was very popular in my small town and, since we only lived two hours from Houston, we went at least once a year to see the rodeo and the live entertainment that was booked for that season.

I remember the Elvis Presley concert that year the most. I was only in third grade, but I knew that night that I was witnessing something special, something life-altering, something…dramatic.

All of a sudden the lights to the Astrodome dimmed and the announcer spoke loudly over the intercom: "Ladies and gentleman, the Houston Astrodome proudly presents…Elvis *Presley*!" The crowd roared, the women screamed, and once everyone sat down I realized what they were screaming about.

There stood Elvis Presley, dark hair, dark smoldering eyes, sexy sideburns, in a white jump suit, with the zipper low enough to give the audience a glimpse of his sexy, hairy chest. I had been to many concerts by that point, and even since, but never felt the sexual energy that Elvis displayed that fateful night.

He was like a power force that exuded sexual energy, almost like electricity. He moved his pelvis and shook his hips in a way that drew the audience in. He sang in a sultry, masculine voice that made you feel like he was singing straight to you. The women in the audience screamed and I could definitely relate to their swooning.

Elvis stirred something in me, even at the tender age of eight. I had never seen a man display sexuality like that before. But something inside of me…*liked*…it. Something inside me stirred. I felt something different. I realize now that I was feeling the same things most of those women were screaming about.

He gave one of the best performances I had ever experienced. He also left me with some big-time questions. I knew that he had stirred something inside of me.

But even at age eight, I innately knew it was something that was better left alone for right now.

Even so I spent my whole allowance and bought his picture book; then I memorized every page. I must have looked at his pictures a million times that year alone. Looking back at my life, that was the first time I remember being attracted to a man: it was third grade, age eight, back at the Houston Astrodome.

I believe that Elvis was my first big crush.

But I couldn't hang his poster on my wall or talk to my friends about swooning over him. I knew that, deep inside. They just wouldn't understand. No one would understand. I also knew that it would be my deepest secret, the one I would keep from the whole world.

Until now…

It may have started with Elvis, but my infatuations soon spread to other men in my small town. There was no particular rhyme or reason to the wavelength of my budding hormones: My coach, my science teacher, a married man in church, all older than me, all very masculine and very sexy.

Needless to say, with no outlet for my emotions, I fantasized a lot. I think that is why I loved television and movies so much; it was a great fantasy escape. The first movie that I ever saw about homosexuality was called *Making Love*.

At the time they made it, I don't believe those actors knew what an escape that movie was for millions of gay men. It was the first time I had ever seen two men kiss. I can't tell you what that was like for me.

It was such a…validation. I finally realized, perhaps for the very first time in my life, that I was not the only one. The movie was done so well and the actors were purely gorgeous.

If you haven't seen the movie, it's a must see. I would later meet Kate Jackson, one of the stars of the movie, in Las Vegas and get her autograph. Let's just say that she was not overly friendly. But she was not the one I was lusting for in the movie anyway, so it really didn't matter.

The next "gay" movie I saw was *Crusin'*.

Unlike *Making Love*, which thrilled me, that movie scared me to death. It was about a serial murderer that preyed on gay men. (Hardly original these days, of course, but groundbreaking back then.)

He would pick up gorgeous gay men and bring them home and murder them. I always wondered if Jeffery Dahmer, the serial killer, saw that movie and possibly viewed it as his inspiration for a crime spree that would cost the lives of dozens of young men, both gay and straight.

Either way, it certainly made me afraid to ever pick up a guy that I didn't know and go home with him. But that fear wouldn't last very long. Movies and television were my life; it was my date on a Saturday night. The TV became my best friend, my confidante, my mentor. I never cared for watching the Superbowl, but the Academy Awards were never missed.

The man that taught me about sex, believe it or not, was Phil Donahue. I watched Phil's talk show daily, mostly because he was the first heterosexual man that ever talked about gays and lesbians as positive and normal human beings. When Donahue put on a dress and did his entire show on cross dressers, I was hooked.

Phil took a chance and went against the norm about gay rights and AIDS long before it was the fashionable thing to do. Phil Donahue made me feel like I was not alone, he educated me, he made me believe that I was okay.

Phil Donahue did more for talk television and educating people about human rights than he will ever know. In my opinion, at that time, I didn't think anyone could take his place.

But then came Oprah.

Wow! What can you say? I believe Oprah Winfrey is a presence that only comes along once in a lifetime and I feel honored to have grown with her, lost weight with her, and cried with her.

One show Oprah did that sticks out in my mind was when she first started in daytime television. She traveled on location to a southern town and met with an audience of racists. She was fabulous. There she was, this heavy black woman, facing her fears, and opening a dialogue with these racists.

She was trying to understand prejudice and why they didn't want blacks in their small town. The audience members let her have it; they acted as if they didn't want her there, either.

I was so impressed. I felt Oprah had faced her enemy on that show and walked away making them look exactly like what they all were...*ignorant*! I can still remember her standing in the audience sharing the microphone with audience members and asking them very thought-provoking questions.

But inside I knew how she felt, standing in front of all those people using the N-word right to her face, she felt both scared and outraged at the same time. Throughout my impressionable youth, I would come to know that feeling on a daily basis. I hope I can meet her one day. She made such a difference in my life. Run on Oprah! I will watch anything you do. I love *Beloved* and *The Color Purple*.

The Hollywood community always supported homosexuals, whether it was through AIDS awareness or merely acceptance as individual, creative, passionate people. Hollywood used the big screen to enlighten and help change public opinion, hopefully to further acceptance.

From soap operas to talk shows to the big screen, those groundbreaking actors were like my friends that I never had—and I loved them all. I was probably the only boy in my neighborhood that dreamed of walking down the red carpet and accepting an Academy Award some day.

I even know what my acceptance speech will be. However, I won't share that with you until I accept my award for the movie, ***One American Boy***: *The Dolph Crawford Story.*

You see, I believe you have to dream and sometimes dreams *do* come true. Are you listening, members of the Academy? Okay, so you are probably thinking, "I have bought this book, read a few pages by now, and *still* don't know who Dolph Crawford really is…"

Well, trust me, he will reveal himself soon…and you most likely will never forget him.

3

Teenage Wasteland

As I write this chapter, it is Easter Sunday. I spoke with my Mom just this morning. She was getting ready to go to my brother Charlie's house to celebrate Easter. I told her that as she celebrates the day, she should look around the room and take note of her children, her grandchildren, and even her great grandchildren.

I wanted her to look closely at their faces and remember that they are her legacy; after she is gone a bit of her will still live on from generation to generation through her extended family. I explained to her that that is one of the reasons that I decided to write my book.

I, unlike her, will have no children; when I die I will not be surrounded by my children or grandchildren. There will be no one left behind to carry on my legacy, share my genes, or even tell my story...

For that reason I chose to write a book about my life.

A book that will hopefully end up on a library or bookstore bookshelf someday. And on any given day a young man or woman who is struggling with who they are, feeling left out, used up, tossed aside, afraid, or abused, can pick it up and read it and, hopefully, see themselves inside its two hundred or so pages. I hope that they will learn from my experiences, but most importantly I hope that they realize they are not alone.

In a universal way, I suppose, *they* are my children...

I want them to understand that suffering exists in this life, that much is true. But if you're comfortable with who you are, if you can walk around in your own skin and feel like it's a good fit, if you can hold your head up high and be proud of who you are, just like you are, you can survive just about anything.

I have stood before the heterosexual males and their old boy's club and been beat up, spit on, kicked around, cussed out, and even had a gun held to my head. I survived. I walked away.

I live on to tell the story...

I explained to my Mom that my book was about my life and that, although it would be controversial, it would hopefully evoke change in our country and eventually our world. My mother's response to me was: "I guess I don't truly know much about you or your life."

Then the conversation changed, ever so subtly, and, in her own way, my Mom was letting me know that she really didn't want to know anything more about my life. Remember: she was not equipped to raise a homosexual son. That just didn't happen in Bridge City, Texas.

Not now.

Maybe not ever.

I love her for loving me, but now I must ask myself: Does she really even know me at all?

Then again, do I really know...*myself?*

I sure didn't know myself when I was fifteen, that's for sure. I guess it should come as no surprise that my teen years were difficult. It's just the law of averages, I suppose: 30 heteros and one homo in each class and, year after year, the side effects start to build up.

It's like arsenic poisoning: you might not get sick all at once, you might not even notice that you're slowly dying, but eventually the poisonous residue builds up and you wind up flat on your back and fighting for your life.

Not surprisingly, I couldn't really relate to my peers. I felt like I was an alien that had been literally dropped into this world full of heterosexuals, like maybe I had been dumped onto the wrong planet or something.

Everything looked...different...to me.

It wasn't just about wondering why Superbowl Sunday was more important to my pals than the Oscars. The differences seeped into daily life. All day, every day. They looked at girls the way I looked at guys. They thought things were funny that I thought were stupid, and vice versa.

I learned to censure what I said. Instead of saying, "Wow, those flowers sure are pretty," I had to stop myself before I got a good ass whooping. Before I remarked about some article I'd read in one of Mom's magazines about diet or fitness, I had to remember that all my buddies read were *Mad* magazine.

I tried marching to the same drummer as everybody else, I really did. But no matter how hard I tried, I just couldn't walk the so-called straight and narrow. I went left, they went right. I wore black, they wore red.

I didn't try to stand out, not really.

I didn't *try* to be different, it was just written in my bones. I'd be walking around, doing something perfectly natural, look up, and realize everyone was staring at me, wondering, silently, "What is it about that guy? Why is he so different?"

Not that I didn't try to hide it…

To keep myself occupied, I got a job at fifteen and went to school and worked every day from then on. My goal was to save my money and move away from this small town, this alien planet I inhabited where cows and football and cars and pussy were the only things anybody could ever bring themselves to talk about.

Many was the time I found respect for someone. A teacher, say. Or a friend of my father's or a shopkeeper or clerk. I'd look up to them, respect them, think that I'd finally found a person to talk to, to look up to, to emulate.

And then, inevitably, they'd show their ass by laughing at some dumb dirty joke or talking about "niggers" or spitting tobacco on my new jeans or making lewd comments about the town librarian.

Then I'd be all alone again…

There I was, fifteen-years-old, hormones bubbling over like baked beans at a good, old-fashioned Texas cookout, and I'm standing smack dab in the middle of Bridge City. While other boys talked about tits and ass, I grew slowly tired of fake smiling and joining in with inane comments that neither made sense nor fit my skin.

Eventually my sexual arousal for men slowly grew stronger, but I wasn't about to act on it. I was too afraid my secret would get out. So afraid I had to consciously stop myself from looking at men to keep from being tempted.

I grew paranoid, sure that, at any moment, someone was going to discover my deepest desires, look into my heart and see the lust written there. Living in a small town, everyone knew your business and, if they didn't yet, they would soon find it out.

Finally, I got up the courage to talk to my priest, Father Vincent. I went to his house and had a meeting with him. After twenty minutes of making small talk, I finally confessed that I had "impure thoughts for men."

Just my luck, this priest was *not* one of the gay ones. In fact, just the opposite was true; he was totally old-school. After hearing him rant and rave about how "homosexuality was a sin" and "an abomination against God" and that I needed to "repent and free my self from the devil's grasp," I gave in, said 10 Hail Mary's, and got the hell out of there. I was a teenager, all alone, with no one like me in sight, and had no one to whom I could confide my secret.

The sexual urges got stronger…and I got weaker.

Growing up in a small town in Texas was very difficult. Especially in the 60s and 70s, when there was no *Will and Grace,* no *Queer as Folk,* no *Queer Eye for the Straight Guy,* no *Ellen.*

There were, however, rest areas, public parks, dark, humid back rooms in adult book stores, and "glory holes" in public restrooms. For the hetero reader, a glory hole is a hole in the partition between two stalls of a men's restroom. You may have seen them before and wondered what in the hell you were looking at.

Well, now you know…

It's a discreet, if not exactly hygienic, way for men to perform oral sex and still stay in separate stalls, anonymous and distant. (I always wondered who the person was who drilled the holes in the first place. And when? And how?)

I know that Jerry Falwell will have a field day with excerpts like this. I am sure I will be quoted on CBN and TBN. But it is part of my reality, not that I am proud of it. But, back then, it was just what you did when you lived in a small town in Texas and you were, for lack of a better term, horny.

I remember my brother telling me about the rest areas off of I-10, although not in a conspiratorial way to help me relieve some of my pent-up sexual pressure and encourage my sexual identity.

Far from it: he was repulsed by it.

He couldn't believe that "fags" hung out in a dark rest area park and had sex in the bathrooms. Well, even as I nodded and grunted and said, "Uh huh, gross, no way, far out," I quickly made a mental note of this information and, as soon as I got my driver's license, that was the very first place I went.

It was scary at first.

Remember, the movie *Cruisin'* was still firmly etched in my very impressionable small town memory. I assumed that at any moment I would be snuffed out by some serial sex killer preying on gay men at darkened rest area parks just like the one I was visiting. And yet, still I went.

Ah, the power of teenage hormones…

At first I just parked my car in the rest area parking lot. I sat there and watched. That's all I did. I saw men, mostly older men, walking around looking in the windows of my car. They would make eye contact with me and then want me to follow them into the restroom. I was too nervous. I couldn't do it. Besides, none of the men that I saw that first night were attractive enough for me to want to be with sexually.

But it was the beginning of an addiction that would consume me for months to come. I would go there on many late nights from that day forward, usually after I got off from work. I would just sit there and watch; it intrigued me…but never enough to leave the safety of my car and actually experience the "glory" of any of those so-called glory holes.

By now I finally had my first job. Since I wasn't great in sports of any kind, my parents suggested I get the job to "keep busy." Idle hands, and all. While most of the guys my age worked at "Market Basket," a local grocery store, where they spent the days stocking canned corn and scoping out the local talent as it sashayed up and down the bread aisles in high heels and short skirts, I wanted to be different. I had heard that the local pharmacy, "King's Pharmacy," was hiring.

At the time, it was the largest pharmacy in the area. So I got my Mom to drive me down to put in my application. Like many other times during that period of my life, I remember being so nervous and yet so excited at the same time.

I filled out the application the best I could. I didn't have much work experience. I had only worked with my Uncle over the summer shrimping in the Gulf, but I didn't think that was going to win me *this* kind of job. I also had to lie about my age because the job called for a sixteen-year-old with a driver's license.

At the time, I was only fifteen and had just gotten my learner's permit, which permitted me to drive, but only when I was accompanied by a licensed driver. Well, like I had to do so many times in my life, I pretended I was sixteen and very mature and very experienced. I met with the owner, Phil. He talked with me and I must have given a great performance because he hired me on the spot.

I would be the new King's Pharmacy delivery boy, taking prescriptions to the local residents. The fact that I didn't have a driver's license or wasn't old enough to take the job escaped me when I accepted the position. Phil told me to start after school the next day. I was really excited.

I finally had a job.

One more step to freedom. I would be able to make my own money, get me a car, and finally be able to drive over that "Rainbow Bridge" to freedom, acceptance, and hopefully companionship somewhere out there in the bigger world beyond Bridge City, where I was busy marinating in a stew of insecurity, self-doubt, and thanks to folks like Father Vincent, self-hatred.

I subconsciously had it all figured out. I would lie in bed at night and ask God to either change me into a heterosexual male or help me get out of this small town. I didn't really care which one He chose at that point, whichever came first!

I left it in God's hands, since Father Vincent had been no help and, what's worse, had convinced me that I was committing a mortal sin every time I even thought about being with another man.

Even though I was going over Father Vincent's head in the divine chain of command, it didn't really matter because, in my mind, God wasn't going to change my sexuality, anyway. He (or She) had chosen to score me a job and help me get out of this small town instead.

So with no driver's license, I started at King's and never looked back. In the words of Joan Crawford in her classic biopic, *Mommy Dearest*: "Tear down that bitch of a wall and put a window where it ought to be!"

That was my mantra.

Obstacles, these petty things were, only obstacles. No matter what, I was determined to make it out of Bridge City, Texas, either driving over the Rainbow Bridge and never looking back or jumping off the bridge like so many had done before me.

Those were my only two choices in my mind at fifteen and a half, with no driver's license and an application with enough lies and half-truths to get me arrested if Phil ever looked closely enough

Lucky for me, he never did…

Turns out the cloud had a silver lining: Working at King's was the best job I ever had. (Of course, it was also my first, but who's counting?) I would look forward to getting out of school every day and going to work.

The people I worked with were some real characters, mostly women, as the only male was the pharmacist-slash-owner, Phil. He would end up being the first hetero-male I would ever tell that I was homosexual. Bless his heart, he told me that "it didn't matter" and that "he loved me anyway."

That occurred after I had been there for five years. During that time, I was Phil's right hand man. I would help him fill prescriptions, I would talk to doctors on the phone, and I would deliver prescriptions to the local residents, mostly senior citizens who were homebound or lacking transportation. I loved it.

The customers would invite me in for a Coke and a visit. I got to know them all after awhile. Remember, Bridge City only had about 8,000 residents at the time and everybody knew everybody.

The folks I brought prescriptions to were lonely and I was the one person from the outside who could brighten their day. Family was unreliable, their friends were in the same boat, but that boy from King's was always Johnny on the spot!

It was a scene straight out of Mayberry, RFD, played out every day after school. "Come on in, Johnny," they'd say as I stepped into the eternal aroma of mothballs and stale slippers.

"My but don't you look hot," they'd observe, already heading for the icebox and the glass that had probably been sitting out all day, just waiting for me to arrive. "Why don't you set a spell and let me get you a tall glass of ice cold lemonade. By the way, did I ever tell you the story of how I met my husband, the war hero? Don't believe that I did. Well, the year was..."

Even at fifteen years of age, I already had compassion for people who were sad or sick or depressed. (Why wouldn't I? I sure knew where they were coming from.) Phil convinced me to consider the pharmacy as a career. He told me that I was really "a natural" and that I should start thinking about college and he would even help me get my degree, if that's what it took.

At the time, it sure sounded like the thing to do. I knew I wanted to leave Bridge City, but if I could postpone it just a little while longer—just a little while, I kept telling myself—then I could get a degree and have an established career in pharmacy by the time I finally left.

Sounded perfect, and I knew it would be an easy transition, since I was already filling prescriptions anyway. All you really had to do was know how to count, measure, and read a doctor's chicken scratch handwriting.

I don't know why you needed a special degree just for that. Well, like most things in my life, something as seamless as an "easy transition" would never quite factor into the equation of my future happiness.

One day I was working behind the pharmacy counter answering the phones. I had come in early to relieve the daytime delivery person, and I looked up to see a tall blonde, blue eyed, guy that, in my mind, looked exactly like a Polo model.

In my town, that was like winning the good looks lottery, as most of the boys favored Gomer Pyle over Brad Pitt. He had a polished look, strong jaw, dressed nice, and smelled really good. He was definitely *not* what I was used to seeing in this small town pharmacy.

Let alone this small town...

He introduced himself as "David." He needed a refill on Demerol and Tussinex cough syrup. Our eyes met...and I noticed that he held his stare on me for a tad longer than what my Daddy would call "socially acceptable."

I was really nervous.

He saw something in me. I just knew it. Better yet, I *felt* it. He kept looking. I liked that. I wasn't used to being looked at. Not in a good way, anyway. But I was shy, and he was a good ten years older than me. Still, there was something about him. I just couldn't put my finger on it.

Yet...

Later that weekend I got off work late and went to the rest area to see what was happening in my secret little world that only happened in the dark of night and on the edge of town. It was funny to think how differently the rest area looked in the sunlight, where I had stopped with my parents coming to or from a dozen or more family vacations.

Little did they know the sexual carnival they escaped once the sun set. I really had to go to the rest room and so, breaking my usual rule of never leaving the car, I instead waited until I knew that there was no one in the restroom and made a mad dash for it.

By this time all the old guys that hung out in the park knew that I was not into any of them. I had finally talked to several of them over the years. But, to my surprise, they respected that I was not into anything else.

On this night, however, I went straight to the first urinal. The lights were very bright in the restroom at night. It was a cool spring evening. Suddenly, I noticed a clean smell of cologne that I knew I had smelled…somewhere…before. As I was just about to zip up and leave I looked up and…there he stood.

It was David, the Demerol customer from the pharmacy.

He took one look at me and I just froze. He let out the biggest laugh, which sounded even bigger as it bounced from bathroom tile to bathroom tile in the bright, but otherwise empty, public restroom.

"I knew it," he said, giving me neither compliment nor cut-down. "I knew you had to be gay."

"Ouch!" I thought, "that hurt."

Here I had been keeping my secret for eighteen long years, or so I thought, and now he meets me once—just once—and immediately he knows. Was I slipping? But there was something different about David, too.

He appeared to be the perfect man.

He was very good looking, smart, dressed well, drove a nice car, and appeared to have money. We immediately hit it off. We sat in his car that night and talked for hours. We had so much in common. He was raised in Bridge City, he knew everything I was going through, and yet he was also masculine and carried himself well.

I was so impressed that he had managed to survive for so long in the straight world, apparently without compromising his lifestyle, ideals, or beliefs. But it wasn't a sexual attraction for me. Instead, it was more like respect bordering on awe.

David, to me, was a sign sent straight from above. I was finally being shown that there was a gay man that grew up in Bridge City amongst the same people I did, only ten years earlier.

He had survived; he made it across the Rainbow Bridge and now he had great job at a refinery in the Beaumont area. We were instant friends. I talked with him every day after that, sharing with him things I had never told anyone else.

I talked with him about everything that I was feeling. All of it. With David, I held nothing back. It was so…freeing. He was like my therapist. He asked me one time about my earliest recollection that I was…different.

Without hesitation I asked him if he had seen the Christmas show called *Rudolph, the Red Nose Reindeer.*

"Of course" he replied, "who hasn't seen that?"

"Well," I continued, "in that show there is a place called 'The Land of the Misfits.' On this island, there are toys that are not perfect like the rest. There was a doll with one eye, a train with square wheels, etc. I instantly related to that place and to those toys as a young child. They were different and not like the perfect toys, much like I felt."

David was quiet as he listened, then he put his arm around me and gave me a big hug and told me that I was just "special" and "unique." He told me that I would do "great things in my life."

I believed him.

He was my greatest friend. He was just like a brother to me. There was never any sexual relationship with David and me. We didn't want to take a chance and ruin our friendship.

It turned out we were right: our friendship would last for over fifteen years.

David was the guy who brought me "out." For the heterosexual reader, "out" means when someone shows you the ropes in the gay world, takes you to your first gay bar, and basically schools you on the gay lifestyle. (I guess you could say David picked up where Phil Donahue left off.)

The big city of Houston, the Montrose area, to be exact, housed the first gay establishment I ever walked into. You have to picture it: I had braces, I was about 5' 9," weighed about 130 pounds, and still *looked* fifteen. I was still a little scarred from the movie *Cruisin'*, but David convinced me to walk into my first gay bar, JR's in Houston on Montrose.

This was about two hours away from Bridge City, so at least I wasn't afraid of being seen by anyone who knew me. I was still harboring my little secret from the "People on the Grow" in Bridge City, Texas, but hey…I made it across the Port Arthur Bridge without jumping.

That's really saying something.

And, suddenly, there I was standing in front of a real gay bar. As the door to JR's opened, my life began. I call it "gay puberty," the time that a gay male can finally be who he is and socialize and meet other people he is truly attracted to. As I walked in the bar it was a summer Sunday afternoon and the men where hot and muscular and they were all looking at me.

I had never had a man cruise me before and it was exciting, powerful, and scary all at the same time. Remember, I was socialized to believe that lusting for another man was wrong, sick, perverted, and just plain against God.

Well, I'm glad to say that those eighteen solid years of homophobic rhetoric just disappeared as soon as I walked through JR's and finally felt I was *home*.

And I never wanted to leave…

I believe that I was looking for a father figure at that stage of my life. I was very attracted to men who were older than me. I want to digress here and explain that I truly feel that in my case I was *born* homosexual: something happened in the womb and at the point of sexual identity development, mine was simply coded to be attracted to men.

It had nothing to do with a domineering mother or strict father. I wasn't abused or molested or shown Shirley Temple movies in a locked basement for hours at a time. I was born homosexual; it's who I am and what my destiny in this life was supposed to be. I feel like I have to add that for the Jerry Falwells out there who believe that homosexuality is a "choice."

It's not; it's who I am and it's being true to my soul and existence on this earth plane. All right, let me step down off my soapbox now and get back to the juicy stuff: I was overwhelmed by these muscular, gorgeous men with huge biceps and great asses. The song "It's Raining Men" by the Weather Girls was popular then and very appropriate to my first walk through JR's bar.

The mood was open, the atmosphere refreshing, the air charged with that particular scent of sexual tension. Though it was foreign to me, I picked up on it immediately and felt a sudden…shift.

I can't tell you how freeing it was, just to stand there and…breathe. The sexual charge was gratifying, don't get me wrong, and the expectation of what might happen next had my heart racing and my palms clamming. But more than anything I just wanted to stand there and soak up the camaraderie, the potential, the friendship, the acceptance.

Finally, I had found my Land of Misfit Toys…

David was so cool and knew just what to do.

I was awkward and had braces, enough said.

David would just walk up to a guy that he liked and start talking and laughing and was so confident. And there I was, chock full of Catholic guilt and a massive dose of Texas paranoia, like the straight Vice Squad was going to barge through the door any minute and bust me and it would be in all the papers back home.

I didn't have a clue about how to handle myself in a bar—did I mention I had *braces*? I was determined to get rid of that space between my two front teeth; my father would tell me to just "squeeze them between my fingers" and they would move and grow together. My mother looked on the bright side and assured me that Lauren Hutton had a space between her teeth and "just look how successful she was."

Well, gay as I was I *still* didn't want to be Lauren Hutton, so I got braces at eighteen, just another obstacle on my road from awkward duckling to graceful swan. Despite my misgivings, I finally broke away from David at JR's and began to cruise the club on my own.

I was like a kid in a candy store, alternating from bashful stares at my squeaky tennis shoes to furtive glances at the approving smiles of the handsome men I passed along the way. They crowded the barstools like window dressing, a veritable buffet of good-looking men just waiting for me to choose one.

As I finally made my way to the back bar I saw a gorgeous, tall, muscular man that was surrounded by other good looking men, but somehow he just stood out as the leader of the group.

I was instantly in love.

I found a spot to stand in so I could stare at him without looking like a stalker. It was great; I couldn't wait to tell David all about him. When David finally found me the bar was clearing out but "my man" was still there. I hadn't taken my eyes off of him for all that time.

I filled David in on the man that I was in love with. And, unbelievably, without hesitation, David just walked up to where my future boyfriend was standing and started talking…to…him.

I was impressed.

The next thing I knew, David and the gorgeous guy were looking in my direction. I got nervous and turned away. But before I could walk away my dream man was standing right in front of me.

He looked like a Greek statue, with his long, lean, muscular body and a chiseled face. I had never had a relationship with a man and didn't have a clue about what I was doing.

Craig was his name; he was a male nurse. He was the one who taught me about safe sex. Of course, the only concern at that time was hepatitis or VD. HIV wasn't known about—yet—but there *was* a "mysterious disease" that was being talked about in New York City.

But to me, New York seemed a million miles away…

At first, it was difficult for me to be intimate with a man. I had to have a few drinks to be sexual and, afterward, I couldn't wait to leave. Remember, I didn't have a role model to follow and I felt that Catholic guilt, so…what did I do? I ran. Straight back over the Port Arthur Bridge.

Back in Bridge City, I felt like a different person.

I wanted to feel alive again, and the gay bars of the Montrose district called to me from afar. Unfortunately, my job was in Bridge City and, on top of that, I was attending Lamar University for pre-pharmacy. After that first walk through JR's, though, I just couldn't concentrate on school anymore.

I literally felt as if I couldn't breathe in that town. My grades began to fall. It was no mystery; my heart was no longer in it. I would eventually quit college altogether shortly thereafter.

Something inside of me wanted to immerse myself in the gay lifestyle and the Big City was calling my name. I wanted to move to a city that had a big gay population. I'd been to the mountaintop, now I was back down at base camp!

I wanted to lace up my boots and scale the Mt. Everest of gay life…

I convinced Scoop, my best friend at the time, to strike out with me and travel to Austin, the biggest Big City we could find. He and I struck out, all right, but Scoop was still in the closet and, although I sensed he was probably gay, I didn't want him to know my secret yet, either.

I was too afraid that I might lose him as a friend.

Eventually, Scoop came out to me and I, in turn, told him about my Houston experience. Scoop's Uncle John lived in Houston, so at least we had a place to stay when we'd roll into town, my car pulling in on gas fumes. Even better: Uncle John was gay. It was like leaving the hetero-desert and winding up in the homo Promised Land!

Uncle John was a character; he worked as a window dresser at a major department store in Houston and he had an obsession with Gene Harlow. Not exactly a role model for two eighteen-year-old Texas boys, but he was a lot of fun and, after all, we weren't your typical Texas boys anyway.

Scoop and I had a great summer in Houston, traveling there almost every weekend. We would leave work on Saturday and drive up for Saturday nights at the bars and Sunday T-dance. It was a blast.

We had no money but, as the resident "young bloods" on the scene, never had to buy drinks once we got there and *always* found someone who would be glad to give us a place to stay.

I must admit I was very promiscuous in the beginning, and I definitely reveled in the attention. As refreshing as it was for Scoop and I to escape the shackles of Bridge City, it was doubly so for these middle-aged gay men to entertain such hot young customers. Still, when a guy wanted me to go home with him I always had to make it clear that my buddy Scoop would have to sleep on the sofa.

Unlike me, Scoop was not promiscuous; he just loved to be out at the bars being surrounded by people who were like him. Although Scoop and I had been best friends since kindergarten, we were never intimate—to me Scoop was like a brother.

We were inseparable, though, and we both loved to laugh and be carefree. It was a friendship that I truly valued and I was truly fortunate that we found each other in Bridge City.

Back at home, my Dad was going through some growing pains of his own and had to make a decision as to whether to retire early and get a lump sum or stay on at the refinery until he was 65. Either way, it was not a good scene for a young gay man testing the waters of independence and growth.

Needless to say, my Dad and I clashed a lot. I was angry and scared and he didn't understand why, at eighteen, in the prime of my sexual youth, I was not dating girls. My mother was the catalyst between us. She loved us both, but she saw that we were not getting along. I would yell, he would yell, he would hit and, once I was big enough, I would hit back.

One morning he woke me up and insisted that I come outside and help him change the oil in my car. I was hungover, but I did what he said. As I got in my car to drive it up on the rack he kept in the garage for just such occasions, I suddenly noticed that a gay magazine that I had placed under my front seat was now lying on the passenger seat…fully exposed.

I froze.

I looked up, and there he stood, looking at me through the car window with knowing eyes and a disapproving expression. He knew! He had seen the magazine! My secret was out. The look on my father's face, as I recall it now so many years ago in crystal clear retro-vision, was one of total…*disgust.*

He was extremely disappointed in his only natural son.

I knew I had to get away from him, immediately, so I just took off running. It wasn't exactly the most grown-up reaction in the world, I'll admit, but I felt I had no choice at the moment. It was like a grenade had just been dropped and I was the only one with sense enough to head for the hills!

He shouted after me: "We need to talk about this!"

When I was at a comfortable distance away from him I shouted back: "It's too late to talk!"

At that moment, we both knew that our relationship was over.

You see, I was embarrassed that my Dad knew my secret and I knew he was never going to approve of my lifestyle. Looking back now, I believe that my Dad knew he could no longer protect me anymore.

Furthermore, he knew the road I had chosen for myself, my path as a gay man in a small town, was going to be tougher than it would be for the average boy from Bridge City, because I was growing up in an area that, in his mind, was dangerous and unacceptable by most standards. The last thing he shouted as we stood at opposite sides of the property was, "Let's not tell your mother about this."

That was fine with me.

I didn't want to share my secret with anyone, let alone my poor mother, but unfortunately now my Dad knew. As always in my life, I made the best of things. I would work hard at the pharmacy all week and play a good straight boy role for the sake of my family.

But as soon as the weekend came, the gay bars would be calling me like a lonesome, randy cowboy on a long, hot cattle drive. It was an interesting dichotomy: on one hand I was working—and by all accounts succeeding—in the hetero-world and on the other I was playing it to the hilt in the homo-world.

I remember each time I drove back to Bridge City from Houston, a part of me slowly changed and soon I knew that I would have to make a decision. I knew that my being different would be a reflection on my family and I didn't want them to suffer that in a small town like Bridge City.

So I would have to make a decision.

A big one…

Well, as has happened so often in my life, that decision was soon made for me. As I said before, my Dad decided to retire from the refinery and, all of a sudden, he was around the house a lot.

A *whole* lot.

The more we were around each other, unfortunately, the more we fought. It finally came to a head one day. I was on the phone talking to my friend, David, who I talked to almost every day.

Suddenly, my Dad came in my room and told me to "get off the phone" and follow him while he drove his father, Whistler, home. (We nicknamed my grandfather "Whistler," because toward the end of his life he developed a nervous whistle.)

Well, apparently I didn't get off the phone quick enough for my Dad because the next thing I knew he was up in my face yelling and screaming for me to get off the phone—immediately!

I got off the phone, all right, and as calmly as possible I advised my father to "never to talk to me like a dog" and that I was "not going to put up with his yelling and screaming."

Apparently, that was not the right answer and he yelled at me all the way into the driveway. It finally came to blows. That was pretty normal between my Dad and me; we knew how to push each other's buttons.

But this time it was different, because as we fought in the driveway my sister and her husband happened to pull up. Then my grandmother, who lived next door, came outside and soon my mother came running out of the house as well.

It must have looked like a scene straight out of the Hatfields and the McCoys!

I believe that, to them, it looked as if the big showdown between us was going to explode and it was not going to be good in the end. As my Dad had me against the car and was slapping me around his father, Whistler, got out of the car and yelled at my Dad, his own son.

That was when everything…just…stopped.

My Dad looked dazed and, for a split second, I saw him as a little boy getting scolded by *his* father. Everyone stood still in time, at least for that one split second. Then my Dad simply let go of me and walked away.

It was like all the wind had just gotten knocked out of his sails and there was nothing left anymore. Like the marionette who'd been pulling his strings just held up his hands and said, "That's it, I can't do this anymore."

Almost like he just gave up…

Whistler got back in the car and I drove him home.

Then I patiently waited for someone to pick me up at Whistler's house. Assuming it was going to be my Dad, I was surprised when I saw Dana, my sister, and her husband pull up instead. Now, remember, I looked at Dana as my ally. My confident. My trusted friend.

So I was devastated when I got in the car and she turned to me and said, "You need to move out of Mom and Dad's house; you're causing too much trouble." In my mind, at that time anyway, it was "me against them." I was an outsider and, as such, I would need to leave.

As I said before my Grandmother, Effie, lived next door to Mom and Dad in a mobile home. Effie was a character. She had long blonde hair, long fingernails, and wore split skirts and nylons with seams down the back. A perfect "fag hag" if ever there was one.

She was so good to me and I, in turn, always tried to be good to her. So I escaped to her house and told her my dilemma. She told me she was shocked by the altercation between my Dad and me, but she never took sides; she loved us both.

When I told her I was gay all she said was, "Honey, let me tell you one damn thing: you could run neked outside and I would still love you…Grandma don't give a big rat's ass what people think as long as *you* know who *you* are."

I needed to hear that.

But what I really needed was a plan for how to leave Bridge City, because my Grandmother lived on my Dad's property and I didn't want to cause a conflict between them. Well, Effie must have been thinking the same thing because later that week she told my Uncle and his wife, Glenda, what happened and Glenda saved the day.

It seemed as if Glenda's daughter, Sandy, was a flight attendant for American Eagle airlines, and it just so happened that they were hiring flight attendants. Glenda got me an application from Sandy and I filled it out and two weeks later I got a letter stating that I had an interview in Dallas.

4

The Air Up There

Finally, my small town was behind me.

I had crossed over the Rainbow Bridge and now I was sitting on a plane headed to the big city of Dallas, Texas. I remember seeing the Dallas skyline for the first time...it was beautifully lit with multi-colored lights, the Reunion Tower ball glittering in the background.

I was finally able to exhale as the plane touched down at Dallas-Forth Worth Airport. I had finally arrived in a big city. A city where no one knew me. A city that was big enough to get lost in. To lose oneself in new people, new opportunities, new experience, new attitudes...a new life.

Around me on the plane weary business travelers and expectant tourists went about the routine debarkation, scrambling to baggage claim and quickly grabbing their briefcases or backpacks full of suntan lotion. But for me it was a different feeling: an act of emancipation.

I was...free.

Or was I?

It was so surreal; I had finally escaped my small town, but I knew that was just the beginning of a daunting new experience that could send me packing just as quickly as it could send me skyward.

I would still have to win the airline over at the interview. But I knew I could always rely on my inherent acting skills and I felt surprisingly confident as I grabbed my humble looking luggage off of the revolving baggage carousel.

All that changed when I arrived at the flight attendant interview, where I was overwhelmed by the massive and intimidating crowd. There must have been two hundred people interviewing that day from all over the country, out of which I knew less than fifty would be selected for the job. As I had expected, the group was comprised of mostly girls, but there were a few guys there was well, maybe fifteen out of the assembled 200.

For once it felt good to be in the minority: The rumor was that American Eagle (then called Metro Airlines) was needing to hire at least one guy in response to some quota handed down from the head office. At least my odds were somewhat better than the girls.

But not by far.

Most of the people there had just graduated from flight attendant school. (I didn't know that even existed, a school for flight attendants.) It began to dawn on me how naïve I'd been to head out from the sticks all the way to the big city, pinning my dreams on a job it now seemed I had little hope of getting.

But that's how desperate I was to get out of Bridge City.

The flight attendant school grads were all very stylish, and they knew it. They had been taught how to interview with major companies. They were very polished. They were all dressed in navy blue suits with matching shoes and perfectly coiffed hair and flawless make up.

The guys all looked the same…minus the makeup.

They all carried leather briefcases that contained their perfectly documented resumes and freshly printed diplomas from the flight attendant academy. I was in awe of how they were so prepared.

I just knew they would all be hired…and so did they.

Pan back to me: There I sat there in my brown suit, newly purchased from the Sears and Roebuck sales rack. My shoes were newly polished. Newly polished church shoes, that is. My suitcase—forget about anything as fancy as a briefcase—was lime green and one of the zippers was broken. My resume, such as it was, was a single typed piece of paper outlining my years at King's Pharmacy and my one summer of shrimping with my uncle.

Not surprisingly, I began to sweat.

Profusely…

"What the hell am I thinking?" I thought as I sat amongst the airline Barbies and Kens. I didn't have a chance against these flight academy clones. I didn't have a leather briefcase, I had a brown envelope.

I didn't have perfectly coiffed hair, I had a cowlick in the back of my head that despite my best attempts at calming it down with everything from hair goop to spit and the back of my hand was being quite uncooperative that day.

As luck would have it, on the flight from Beaumont to Dallas, I had met a few girls from my area that were interviewing for the same position: Crystal, Lacy, Rebecca, and Kim. It was like an airline version of the hit TV show, *Three's Company*! (Guess who was Jack?)

We got acquainted on the plane so naturally we hung out together during the interview process. Despite our newfound friendship, however, I was still determined to lose them once we got to the interview if, by chance, there were any cute guys.

Well, they stuck to me like glue, but that was okay with me because the guys that were attending the interview were definitely *not* my type anyway. As luck would have it, they brought all five of us into the group interview and interviewed us all together. The woman conducting the interview inspected us closely. She especially kept a keen eye on me, but I suppose that was to be expected.

At one point during our one-on-one session I caught a look at myself in the mirror and noticed that my cowlick was sticking straight up. Again. I tried to smooth it down—*again*—when I didn't think she was looking, but she caught me.

I felt like Alfalfa in one of those *Little Rascals* movies. I finally just relaxed and acted more like myself, answering her questions with honesty and responding without pretense.

I knew I stuck out in my brown suit in this ocean of navy blazers. I might as well have had Sears and Roebuck stamped on my sweaty forehead. I was the living, walking, breathing epitome of "country come to town." The problem was I didn't want to return to the country.

I had been in the big city one day and already I didn't want to leave.

After we all interviewed it was time for the airline executives to make their decisions. The academy graduates sat up front in their power suits with their bottled water.

My new friends from Beaumont and I were stuck in the back of the hotel conference room clutching our little resumes and already dreading the flight back to our small towns.

I could hear my Dad now: "I told you so…who the hell wants a man handing them their Coke and peanuts anyhow?"

The woman who interviewed me was introduced as the Vice President of the company. I watched as she approached the podium. She was an older lady with a kind face. Had she been impressed? Unimpressed?

Dazzled, or disappointed?

Kind as it was, her face was impossible to interpret as she began to read off the list of selected flight attendants. There would be thirty flight attendants hired for the next training class.

Would I be one of them?

From the beginning, it didn't look that way.

As predicted, the airline VP started reading names and the girls in the blue blazers and leather briefcases jumped up and screamed and hugged each other and quickly walked to the front of the room to collect their flight attendant school packets before turning around and looking at the rest of us as if we were something they'd just stepped in.

Predictably, she had chosen the first twenty-five girls who had attended flight attendant school. With five more openings left, my group of girls and I were beginning to mentally prepare for the return flight back to Beaumont, to our minimum wage jobs and our disappointed parents and our pipe dreams of making it out of our small towns.

Then the woman called the next four names: Crystal, Lacy, Rebecca, and Kim! All the girls in my group! I was so happy for them! I could sense the confusion from the fleet of navy suits and dye jobs still seated around the room.

I was so proud of my girls.

I knew where they came from and I knew this was their ticket out. Then, with one opening left, the airline VP gave a short speech about how this was American Eagle's first time to hire a male flight attendant…she explained that it would take a "special male" to prevail over all the obstacles that would inevitably befall him.

She explained that all the major carriers hired men and that "…now it was time that American Eagle follow the ranks of the other major airlines."

The guys in their identical navy suits sat up straight, mentally preparing themselves to accept the position. Then the woman read the final name on the list: It was mine! I felt everything happen in slow motion.

I saw myself falling from that Rainbow Bridge and, ironically, this woman I had never met before that day reached down and pulled me back before I hit the water and sank straight to the bottom.

My girls screamed!

They pushed me out of my seat, without them I would probably still be setting there, to this day, in shock. I was overwhelmed as I accepted the orientation packet and agreed to take my position as first male flight attendant. I couldn't help but believe God had finally come through.

He didn't change my sexuality, that was obvious to me.

But He *did* get me out of my small town…

He gave me a chance to travel and meet new people and find myself and, hopefully, someone like myself to love and share my life with. I quietly thanked God—and the woman who handed me the packet.

I'll never forget how she gently patted my back and said softly: "It won't be an easy task, but I believe you can do it. I think you have what it takes." She then reached up and tousled my cowlick on the back of my head and remarked: "Just be yourself."

I remember thinking: "Yeah, I can finally be myself. I am in a big city now and people here are more educated and forward thinking. They won't care if I am gay." Well, I would soon find out that wasn't the case.

Dallas might have been bigger, but the skies above it were not so "friendly."

For the next month, training school was rigorous but exciting. I was the only male out of thirty females, so I was naturally the center of attention. (Which, if you've been paying attention so far, suited me just fine!)

I stuck pretty close to my gal pals from Beaumont: Crystal, Lacy, Rebecca, and Kim. But, little by little, I got to know some of the other girls in the training class as well. I quickly noticed that the supervisors, Laverne and Debbie, kept a close watch on me throughout the training. I believe they were trying to see if I was going to fit in with the male pilots.

The word was already out on the wire that a male flight attendant had been hired. The rumor was that the pilots were going to do everything they could to make sure I didn't last very long once I came out of training.

I won't say the news didn't disturb me, but I suppose it was to be expected. It was disappointing to make it so far, to leave Bridge City behind, to beat out 170 freshly graduated fight attendant school alumni, to make history, as it were, only to find the same fears, prejudices, and scare tactics abounded just about everywhere else.

"Why had I thought Dallas would be any different?" I wondered. "Or American Eagle, for that matter?"

It was like that old saying, "Wherever you go, there you are."

If I'd thought the grass was going to be any greener in "the air up there," I had certainly been mistaken. Still, I had made it this far and a bunch of overweight, balding airline pilots with their square asses and flat feet weren't going to intimidate me.

The female flight attendants, however, were very curious to see what this new male flight attendant looked like and, of course, the question on everyone's mind was, "Was he gay? Or was he straight?"

I had already leaked the story that I had a "girlfriend" back home and that I was "very committed to our relationship." Some girls thought it was "sweet," while others still questioned it.

The girls from Beaumont felt safe with me and that's all that mattered.

I remember my first day "on the line," meaning going live on an actual airplane flying through the air, my position was still so new that they didn't even have a uniform for me yet.

I had to go to the mall and purchase a button down white shirt and navy pants and black shoes before my shift was to begin. (I chose boots because they made me look taller.)

My supervisor, Laverne, escorted me out to the plane.

I was nervous enough, as anyone would be, but as this was the first flight with a male attendant for the entire airline, the mood in the cockpit was very tense. Laverne would introduce me to the pilots, but they would simply ignore me and talk directly to her, as if I wasn't there

Real mature, guys…

Looking back, it's almost comical now but at the time it was extremely embarrassing. Despite their negative attitudes, however, my flights that day went very smoothly.

I was the only flight attendant amongst 50 passengers. The passengers didn't seem to have a problem with a male flight attendant. So I was comfortable in the cabin, where it really mattered anyway.

Best of all, I loved making my PA announcements.

It was like having an audience to perform for. Unfortunately, while the audience was most certainly captive, they weren't exactly rapt: most people only wanted their peanuts and beverage; they couldn't care less about how to use a seatbelt or where the emergency exit rows were.

Their lax attitude and downcast eyes only gave me the freedom to be all the more creative with my delivery, something that would later stand me in good stead as I entered the acting profession.

Once we got through a month of training and a week of supervised observations, we graduated and were finally on our own. We soon found out that we would be based in Lawton, Oklahoma. There was a large military base there called Lawton-Fort Sill, and most of our fares would be standard pick-ups and drop-offs.

Most people working for the airline rented what were known as "crash pads," where one person gets an apartment and about 10 people crash there at the start and finish of their trips. Most people didn't live in Lawton, but commuted back and forth. I had nowhere else to go, so I decided to get an apartment.

Well, my gal pals from Beaumont wanted to crash at my place, so I readily agreed. We'd been through so much together, why not just make it official and live together, too? Besides, I didn't have a lot of money and they could help with rent.

So there we were in a two bedroom apartment with four girls and me. Every straight man's dream, right? Four beautiful young girls running around the house in bra and panties at all hours of the day or night?

It may have been a straight man's dream, but it was a gay man's *nightmare…*

I flew a lot in the beginning, mostly delivering new recruits into Lawton-Fort Sill. I would pick up the flight at Dallas-Forth Worth airport and take it into Lawton, which was approximately a 45-minute flight.

These poor guys had been on planes all day coming from all over the country and this was the last flight where they would have any kind of freedom because, for them, the next six weeks of basic training were going to be pure hell. I quickly learned that all they wanted at that point in their life was pussy and beer.

Well, I couldn't accommodate them with the pussy part but I could sure keep the beer flowing. And that is exactly what I did. Upon starting every trip I would fill my flight bags with beer.

And lots of it.

As soon as I got on board I would empty the beer in the plane's ice chest. I would have to cover it in ice so that the pilots wouldn't discover it, as the airline had a strict policy against selling anything other than their approved alcoholic beverages, which were generally overpriced miniatures or, as they've come to be known, "airplane bottles." Once the young, impressionable new recruits got on board, I would lock the homophobic pilots in the cockpit and then my show *really* began.

I would tell the recruits that I had ice cold beer for $3 a can. I didn't have any change, so they would have to pool their money to get the beer. They loved it. I would quickly go up and down the aisle serving these guys cold beer and they were happy to have it. Some would even get up and help me because they knew it was only a 45-minute flight and there was fifty of them and only one of me.

Now *that's* every gay man's dream…

I made so much money serving up beer that I was able to pay off most of my bills and actually start to save money for a rainy day. Still, the flying franchise wasn't exactly risk-free.

I remember one time landing in Lawton the captain made a hard landing and beer cans went rolling down the aisles and into the galley. I realized then that I better be more cautious. If the airline knew I wasn't serving their over-priced liquor, I would be fired for sure.

Back at the crash pad my gal pals were being nosy, trying to find out my little secret. Apparently, serving drinks at 30,000-feet wasn't the only thing they were good at. Crystal went snooping through my bags and found a journal that I kept, long before it was the cool thing to do.

In my journal was a letter to one of the men I had met on a flight. It was very intimate and very personal and loaded with more than enough ammunition for Crystal to reveal my "secret."

That evening I was working a flight back to my base in Lawton and my room-mate Kim was dead-heading to Lawton as well. She followed me to the galley and helped me with my drinks. She also told me what Crystal had done. It seemed Crystal wasted no time letting all of my other house mates in on my personal business.

My "secret" was out…

Kim and I both knew it would be just a matter of time before it was known all over the company. I had mixed feelings about the revelation. On one hand I appreciated Kim being honest with me, but I was also angry at my other room-mates for violating my privacy, especially when the revelation could cost me my job. Fortunately, weeks later it was announced that the base would be moving to Dallas.

This was perfect timing, because I no longer had to room with four other people and Dallas was a bigger base so you really didn't see anyone until you flew. But once I flew I realized my secret was now public knowledge.

Nothing was said outright, not exactly, but the feeling was definitely in the air. Literally. It was like after my Dad had found out I was gay; nothing was ever the same between us again.

It's times like those when you really learn who your real friends are, and usually you're left with about half as much as you started with. It was hard, but I managed to take it in stride. It was my burden to bear. If they didn't like me for who I was by now, I no longer cared to try to befriend them, either.

Despite the almost daily tension, I flew for about two years with American Eagle. After a year they finally issued me an airline uniform. I guess they realized I was going to stay awhile. Try as they may, the pilots just couldn't break me. Most of the older guys would give me the cold shoulder.

They wouldn't want me to serve them in the cockpit. They would tell me to keep the door locked, as if the first chance I got I'd be up there flirting and jumping their bones or something like that. As if I couldn't keep my hands off them or something. Like I would be attracted to those old, fat asses, anyway.

For the hetero male reader, I must add a bit of information here: I know that a lot of straight men will have sex with any kind of woman and don't care what she looks like or what her personality is like. However, the gay male is a *little* more discriminating. In fact, most of us are very particular about the kind of male we are attracted to.

In my case, I like a masculine, muscular man with a nice face and sexy smile. I also like a man that is confident and articulate. A man that can talk about more than just football, cars, or working out.

And a man that is not pretentious.

I am here to inform the homophobic, pot-bellied, good ole, redneck bubba: "You have nothing to fear from a queer!" You could walk naked through a gay bar and no one would lay a finger on you.

That's usually the type of men that are picketing gay events with signs that read: "Fags burn in hell," or popping up on a local news show in some country town talking about how homosexuality is a "sin" or an "abomination of God."

To those folks I simply say, "Your hell is on this earth. Because you operate from hate, you are in a constant state of delusion. You're miserable, insecure, and perhaps not truly comfortable with your sexual identity, or else you would have a life."

Anyway, that is what type of pilots I had to deal with on a daily basis. But my upbringing had already prepared me for rednecks, homophobes, and morons, so it wasn't that much of a stretch from the Friday night football games or my homophobic gym teachers.

In all that time the cold shoulder from pilots never got better, actually, it just became tolerable. They didn't want me to meet them for drinks on overnights, which was standard operating procedure with the stewardesses.

But that was fine with me.

I was getting busy in my room counting my money from the beer sales from the previous flights. I took those hetero men's money and brought them 45-minutes of happiness. If the truth be known, I was making more money in liquor sales than the good ole pilots were making stuck in that cockpit together gossiping about me.

But one night all that came to a head.

As usual I was working a flight from Dallas-Forth Worth to Lawton. It was the last flight out. The pilots were in a hurry to finish their shift and commute home. They informed me that I had a full flight and they wanted to board the passengers quickly and get taxied out of DFW before they were put in a hold for take off.

I was adhering to their request and getting passengers seated and luggage stored as quickly as possible. As usual, I began to recite my spiel over the PA when I noticed an elderly black woman leaning over in her seat with her eyes bulging out and sweat pouring from her face. I immediately dropped my microphone and went to see if she was okay. At this time the plane was already taxiing down the runway.

When I reached the elderly passenger, I discovered she was not breathing and possibly experiencing cardiac arrest. I alerted the other passengers to stay calm. I then notified my captain that we "...had to turn back; I had a potential cardiac arrest passenger!" I pulled the woman into the aisle and began CPR. She was cold! She did not respond!

Sensing this, the other passengers began to panic!

I had to keep them calm, continue CPR, *and* access the situation, all at the same time. By this time we were at the gate and the ambulance was on its way. The pilot and the first officer simply sat in the cockpit.

Neither of them offered me any assistance. Finally, the EMS crew arrived on the plane and took over the patient. But I knew they were already too late. The passenger had already died in my arms moments before they arrived.

I remember hearing her take a deep breath and then her body just...relaxed. Almost instantly, her body turned cold. But the look on her face was so serene, it mesmerized me. I remember thinking that wherever she went, it sure must have been peaceful.

As the EMS worked on the passenger, I went up to the cockpit and reported to the captain that I felt the passenger was dead. The captain turned and snapped at me: "Don't say that, the FAA will ground the plane and we will never get to Oklahoma! Get the EMS to get her off the plane and get that door shut!"

So, once again I complied with his order and helped the EMS deplane the passenger and shut the door. After that, I simply worked the flight, as if nothing had ever happened.

The passengers, and I, knew better.

It was the quietest flight I think I ever flew. All the passengers sat there quietly, no one bothered me. They all knew we had just witnessed death and it seemed appropriate to everyone that the next 45 minutes should be in silent memoriam to that nameless dead passenger whose life was snuffed out so quickly and surprisingly.

Once we reached Lawton, I deplaned all the dazed passengers. When I walked through the can I noticed a sweater in the overhead bin. I picked it up and clutched it to my chest!

I knew it belonged to the dead woman, her unmistakable perfume was all over it. I walked into the Lawton airport holding that sweater. When I got off the plane, there was a black man and woman still waiting at the gate.

Waiting, I knew, for a passenger that would never deplane...

As I walked up to them, they immediately identified her sweater. The woman asked me if her mother was on the flight. She saw my face and looked at the sweater and tears filled her eyes.

The airline had not told them yet. I would have to break the news. I couldn't lie to them; I told the couple that the woman had passed away. I told them of her last moments. I told them of her peaceful face.

I told them she didn't suffer...

Then something amazing happened: they hugged me and we wept together. I had never experienced anything like it before. There we were, three strangers. They were mourning the passing of their mother; I was crying for a woman that I didn't even know, but for a soul that I witnessed peacefully leave this earth. I never forgot those people's faces.

I hope I gave them some peace in their moment of need.

The next day I was interviewed by some insurance company. No one asked if I was okay. (This was long before corporate America began giving lip service to anything as touchy-feely as "sensitivity training.") They just wanted to make sure that the company's butt was covered from any lawsuits or investigations the family might instigate.

After that, I realized more than ever that the pilots didn't have my back in an emergency situation. They should have assisted me once the plane was at the gate. That was standard protocol. Instead, I got no help at all. In my mind, I couldn't trust them. It was only then that I finally knew that I would have to move on.

5

The Mayflower Madman

After leaving American Eagle Airlines, I was tired of existing in a hetero-world. I was tired of playing their game. Tired of suppressing who I was. I knew I had to make a decision: I could find a job in Dallas or move back to Bridge City.

I just shuddered at the thought of going back to that small town; I knew I wouldn't grow there, no matter how many times I read that tired old slogan at the city limits. It just wasn't healthy for me emotionally.

And so, at twenty-two-years old, I was living in Dallas with a little money, the tens and fives I had saved for a rainy day. Well, in my mind then it was starting to sprinkle so I would have to find a job—and quickly.

I was ready to experience the gay side of life. Work in a gay atmosphere and really explore that side of my life. So I went to the Oak Lawn area in Dallas. There are many gay bars there, lined up right next to each other, so like a kid in a candy store I just started going down the line. I applied at one club and the manager told me that they were looking for "male dancers."

He said dancers…wink, wink, nudge, nudge…he meant *stripper*.

So I went home and thought about it, checked my bank statement, looked at the pile of bills that was beginning to form on my counter, getting ready to erupt any minute like Mount Vesuvius. It was then that I decided that I would be a dancer. Maybe, I decided, it wouldn't be so bad, after all.

Much like my "performance" on the PA every flight, it would be an opportunity to create a character. I was determined not to be just some nasty, bump and grind, shake your ass for a dollar dancer. I wanted to be a gay version of the famous Chippendale dancers.

As was my habit, I never did anything half-assed.

Not working at King's Pharmacy, where the owner wanted to stake my career as a pharmacist. Not working for the airlines, where I became one of the first male flight attendants.

Not even stripping in a gay bar.

So I started to grow my hair long. I hit the gym. I became engrossed in muscle magazines and supplements to make me bigger. I tanned and pumped iron. By now it was the roaring 80s and I might as well have been cast in Olivia Newton John's video for "Let's Get Physical!"

Within a few months I created my own version of a Chippendale dancer: Lance; that was my dancing name. I remember the first time I walked onstage. It was at the Village Station, a huge two-story dance club in Oak Lawn. The music started, the drag queen introduced me. The spotlight hit me, the crowd cheered, and I was ALIVE! The audience loved it.

Suddenly, I could dance for four hours a night and walk away with enough money to pay my bills and stay in Dallas. I got a lot of attention. I met a lot of people and, for perhaps the first time, I was able to observe gay people interacting in a gay environment on a regular basis.

From my platform I was above the audience, swirling and jiving to the wicked 80s tunes, I had a great view of all the customers that were there each night. All different types of characters.

Much like in straight bars, the gay life is populated by "types."

I noticed very good looking men, with great bodies. There were very masculine men, very feminine men, drag queens, cross dressers, lesbians, feminine and butch. Best of all, I noticed that no one was being judged, laughed at, or beaten up.

In all the time I danced in gay bars, I never saw one fight break out, I never witnessed anyone tearing up or breaking furniture. You didn't have bouncers in gay bars. You didn't need them. There weren't violent people in gay bars. The violent people, it turns out, were on the outside.

And I mean, *right* outside...

As you left the clubs you had to be very cautious because there were always homophobes that preyed on gay people lurking around. Gays were an easy target for a thief. Most gays would not fight back or resist. Even though they would give the mugger the money or jewelry, they were often times beaten or even killed just because they were gay.

The city called these muggings "isolated cases." It wasn't isolated. Most victims just never reported the crime, because they knew that they would have to give an address where the incident occurred. Then it would be public knowledge that they were in a "gay area" of town.

It could cost the victim his or her job, alienation by family members, as well as public humiliation. So they kept their attack secret. Like they kept their sexual identity a secret.

Their love affairs secret.

Their appetites and desires and joys and triumphs in the gay life a secret. Secrets…secrets…dirty little secrets. (In my next book I have many dirty little secrets, but I will leave that for the sequel.)

My point is that if the hetero-world could have had the view that I had while I was dancing up on those risers, to witness descent people enjoying themselves with no fighting or arguments or power or control, just simply having a good time enjoying friends, making new friends, meeting potential mates or lovers, perhaps the hetero-world could incorporate this in their own life.

Straight women over the years have discovered the gay bars and felt more and more comfortable going to gay clubs and dancing and feeling safe and carefree. However, straight men soon followed the straight women.

Now the gay bars are what they call mixed clubs…gay and straight. Now you need bouncers, because suddenly there are fights and drugs are rampant in the clubs. It's not what it was.

But with everything in life, change is inevitable.

I danced nightly in the gay clubs, making money and creating a fantasy for my audience. My character, Lance, was young looking, sexy, and very erotic. Recalling that fateful trip to the Houston Astrodome when I was only eight and first felt the urge to merge with men, I took some tips from Elvis and moved my hips and flexed my chest and the audience loved it.

Dancing was something that gave me confidence, and a sense of power and a great feeling of being loved by the audience. My favorite quote that sums up my dancing experience comes from the musical *Chicago*.

In one pivotal scene Roxie Star says to her audience: "I'm a star and the audience loves me…and I love them…and they love me for loving them…and I love them for loving me…and we love each other…and that's because none of us got enough love in our childhood…and that's showbiz…KIDS!"

Soon, however, dancing was not enough for me.

I was a budding entrepreneur. I knew I was a good entertainer; I had mastered it. I never went home with anyone that knew me as Lance. I felt like that would ruin the fantasy.

It was all business for me. Despite the stereotype of the promiscuous gay male of the pre-AIDS 80s, there were no drugs, no alcohol for me; I had to keep up the Chippendale dancer body. I had seen too many dancers burn out too soon. I was not going to be a statistic.

One night while I was dancing I noticed a dancer that was older than me. He was a tall, good-looking Puerto Rican male. His body was chiseled and ripped. His face was sexy and kind. He had dark, curly hair and green eyes.

His name was Kevin.

I noticed that Kevin stuck out amongst the rest of the dancers I had seen come through the bars. He dressed really nice, he had expensive clothes, and drove a sports car. He was very polished, but sexy, too.

I started to get to know Kevin; there was something about him that fascinated me. Like me, he was all business. He would leave right after the shows and always drew a large crowd. He was friendly, but cautious. He was not promiscuous. He and I hit it off immediately. We would hang out a lot after we got off work.

I soon noticed that his pager was always going off.

He would excuse himself and go use the pay phone. Yes, youngsters, there was a time, not too long ago, in fact, when there were no such thing as cell phones. In those practically prehistoric days, we used these devices known as "pay phones" to make a phone call.

Back then, it cost 10 cents.

Wow, am I dating myself or *what*?

Anyway, Kevin and I continued to grow closer until finally one night we gave into temptation. He was like a stallion in bed. I had never experienced anything like it. He was so good at sex…I wondered how he got such experience.

We were inseparable after that. I couldn't wait to finish a show and get back to his place. We were so compatible and clicked so easily. I started thinking that this might be the one for me.

I noticed that the more I was around Kevin, the more his phones were ringing and he always kept his answering machine's volume turned down so I couldn't hear who these calls were from. But they were constant…coming in at all hours of the day and night. I was really growing to like this guy, but I felt he was keeping a secret from me.

And you know how I feel about dirty little secrets…

Finally, after a show one night, he was acting very jealous because I was spending too much time with this one guy who had been tipping me big all night. I always stopped dancing and talked with my big tippers.

I built a relationship with them, so they always found me wherever I was dancing. But as we had dinner later that night, Kevin made it clear to me that he thought I was flirting a little *too* much with the guy.

I asked him why he cared.

He told me he thought we were in a "committed relationship." I responded that people in committed relationships "don't keep secrets from each other." I let him know that it was important to me that he tell me about all those phone calls.

I demanded to know about the phone calls during all hours of the day and night. He hesitated for a minute, then finally he told me: He was a male escort and those phone calls were clients that would pay him for…companionship.

"What!?" I thought. "How could that be? We have been together most every night for the last month?" Kevin explained that he had taken some time off to spend time with me and that it was "just business."

But I didn't believe him.

I knew that it was more than that. I left the restaurant and drove home alone that night. I needed time to think. I had encountered many hustlers while dancing, and I didn't want to believe that I couldn't see the signs with Kevin. I guess love is blind or, in my case, just plain stupid.

The next night, after I finished my shift at the club, Kevin was there waiting for me. We hadn't spent the night apart since we met, but I needed time to think. After I explained myself, he said that he understood but he wanted us to "talk it out." He didn't want us to be apart another night. We drove together to eat breakfast and I sat there quietly and let Kevin talk.

He explained to me that he had started small with the escorting, mostly meeting clients through his travels as a dancer. Then his business just grew over the years. He told me that it was like going on a date with someone.

"Often times," he explained, "it's just dinner and a movie." In his case, he got to know the client well before anything sexual occurred. "I am in control," he said. "I don't do anything I don't want to do."

He told me that the money was "incredible," at least ten times as much as he made dancing. I asked him why he did it. He told me that he had set a goal for himself and, once he reached his financial goal, he was going to "get out of the business." Then he told me how much he had made so far.

I had to admit, I was astounded at the figure.

He told me that he wanted to continue our relationship, but I would have to accept him and, more importantly, what he did. He was so irresistible and I was so in love…I gave in.

I don't know why, I guess I felt safe with him. He loved me and I was falling in love with him. I told him that I would give us another chance, but warned that the relationship would always come first before his clients.

He agreed.

That summer was magical with Kevin. He would always meet me after my show, we would go to breakfast, go home, have great sex, sleep late, and work out the next day and lay by the pool until it was time to go back to work. The phone calls didn't bother me as much after a while.

I realized it was just business.

One day as we were lying by the pool and it was time for me to get ready to go to work, Kevin turned to me with those big sexy green eyes and said something that truly shocked me, "Why don't you think about escorting?"

"What?" I asked.

To say the least, I was taken by surprise.

Kevin explained, "Well, right now you work six nights a week at the club. You have to put up with all the stuff in the bars, making nice with the big tippers, competing with the catty dancers, worrying about whether or not you're going to get jumped when you leave by some gay bashers. You get off work and you're exhausted. You aren't guaranteed a certain amount of money. You're better than all that."

I had to admit, he was right; you couldn't count on as many tips on a weekday night as you could on the weekends, when the bars were packed with horny guys just itching to tip off a big chunk of their Friday paycheck.

"You're an actor," he pointed out. "You created Lance as a fantasy dancer. You give the audience what they want and it's all fantasy. Well, it's no different from escorting except you work less hours and make more money."

He *did* make more money than me.

A lot more.

"But, Kevin," I replied. "I can't just be intimate with *anyone*. I'm different from you in that way."

"It's not like that," said Kevin, "it's more…classy…than that. With my clients you meet for dinner and drinks and then it goes from there—or it doesn't. They are paying for your companionship, your time, not your body."

That was all fine and good, but it wasn't until he told me what I could make an hour that I finally started to pay attention. I loved that he was such a business-man; to me, Kevin had it all figured out.

I asked, "What if I don't like the client?"

Kevin quickly replied, "Then you don't have sex with him. It's just like a date. Sometimes you click, other times you don't."

"Won't you be jealous?" I asked.

"No, not at all, because I know it's just business. Besides, you're coming home to me." I finally agreed to do a call, just one, to see what it was like. Kevin was delighted. But first, he suggested I change my name.

He didn't think the name I'd chosen for my dancing persona, "Lance," was appropriate for my escort persona. He told me to think of a name that fit the escort character that I wanted to portray. He would set up the appointment for me with an easy client and I could do the appointment on my day off.

I went to work that night and tried to figure out what my new name would be. What best described my new image? At the time, Dolph Lundgren was a hot action star, appearing in movies like *Rocky IV* and the first *Punisher* film. I liked his masculine features and his sexy eyes.

Inspired, I decided "Dolph" would be my first name.

Then I thought about the dramatic side of me; the refined side that enjoyed good books and great movies. "Who best describes drama," I thought to myself, "but…Joan Crawford?" Every queen knows who *she* is. So I put the two together and "Dolph Crawford' was born!

Kevin loved it.

From then on he called me "Dolph Crawford." However, he wasn't done yet: He wanted to make "Dolph" over completely from "Lance." Kevin suggested I cut my long hair short and shave the mustache and start shaving my legs and chest, too.

He thought I had a really "young look" and I should capitalize on that. I listened to him and had a full makeover. When I looked in the mirror I no longer saw myself, or even Lance.

Now I saw Dolph looking back at me.

That's the earliest memory I have of me losing who I was…

I was finally ready for my first booking. I still remember it to this day. We met for dinner. The client was a middle-aged businessman. He was very nice and very respectful. We had dinner at the mansion on Turtle Creek.

I quickly decided that I liked him. Afterward, we went back to his townhouse and, after all the drama I'd built up around the event in my mind, it turned out to be fairly easy. I was done in twenty minutes, tops. I walked away with more money than I could make dancing on a busy weekend.

Suffice it to say, I was hooked…

After that, I started listening to Kevin about every detail of my life, both personally and professionally. He was like my escort guru. A Swami for sex. He coached me on table manners, how to order the correct wine with dinner, which was the salad fork and which was for the entree.

I must tell you a funny story about my first dinner date. When I read the menu at this fine dining restaurant, it listed a chicken dish "with white wine." Like a value meal, right? I ordered the chicken dish and when the waiter asked me what type of wine I wanted, I replied, "I will just have the white wine that comes with the meal."

The waiter looked puzzled.

Then my client started laughing and explained that the white wine was actually *added* to the chicken in the recipe, like an ingredient, and that it wasn't a glass of wine that came with the dish like some barbecue combo. I was embarrassed and tried to act cool, but I knew I looked like an idiot. I still chuckle about how naïve I was.

About everything.

It was a Jessica Simpson moment, to be sure…

Meanwhile, the money came pouring in. I was shaping up to be Kevin's perfect protégé. I listened to him carefully and, in turn, he molded me into the perfect gentlemen. He taught me how to dress in fine suits, wear expensive shoes and, most importantly, have an expensive watch.

This was of vital importance to Kevin, as he'd learned over the years that watches were the ultimate test of class. "Anyone can lease a Mercedes for a couple of hundred dollars per week," he admonished. "And even *you* can fake your way through ordering the right wine with dinner. But a watch? They don't rent those out and it takes a special man to buy the right watch. It's like a resume in silver and gold."

He was right.

To this day the first thing I notice on a guy is his watch…

When he wasn't schooling me in all things timepiece, Kevin cooked for me, and introduced me to French cuisine and educated me on foreign foods and proper etiquette. He was a great teacher and I was an eager student.

I got so busy with the escorting service, and the physical, mental, emotional, and social upkeep that Kevin demanded, that I had to quit dancing altogether. Surprisingly, I never missed it. Besides, no one even recognized me anymore after Dolph's new transformation.

I was loving the money, Kevin and I were closer than ever, and everything seemed perfect. We worked, we traveled, we shopped. We could walk in a mall or a gym and turn heads. I was so in love and so proud to be with Kevin.

Even so, I was still sure Kevin was hiding something from me. During sex, which was still great, by the way, he never wanted to have anal sex. He was very adamant about that. He didn't want to give or receive anal sex. He was open to anything else…and I mean *anything* else…but NO PENTRATION! He made that very clear to me. It was almost like an obsession with him.

He was a great lover, don't get me wrong, but I just couldn't figure out why he was so stuck on that one particular issue. It's not such a little issue either, believe me. When you're a gay man, there are only so many holes to go around!

All joking aside, I still sensed he was hiding something from me. But I didn't pursue it. After all, we were so busy we barely had time for each other, remember we were still newlyweds.

The business grew and for once Kevin and I could no longer accommodate all the business ourselves. So we decided to hire some more guys and "spread the wealth," so to speak.

It was easy to do; we both knew guys from the dance circuit. By now it had gotten around town what we were doing and many guys were eager to make big money. So an escort service was born.

Kevin and I took turns answering the phones and booking the appointments. Much as I had been only months earlier, the new guys were immediately coached and polished by Kevin.

Sometimes it made me jealous.

The one thing you learn very quickly when your body is a commodity, an asset, is that no matter how young, handsome, and buffed you are, there is always someone younger, more handsome, and in better shape than you.

To watch Kevin take these new guys, "wet clay," he called them, and turn them into little "Mini Me's," just like Kevin, sometimes made me fear for my place in the pecking order.

Still, business was business and there was only so much of Kevin and I to go around. Hiring new boys was just part of the job. And so they were polished into gentlemen, just the way Kevin thought it should be. In the process, he became even more bossy and controlling.

When the book *The Mayflower Madam* by Sydney Biddle Barrows was released, Kevin read it and immediately became obsessed with how she ran her business. It wasn't enough that Kevin read, then re-read it, as often as possible.

He made all the other escorts read it, too.

Basically, it's about an aristocratic madam who runs a high dollar escort service. In the book, she gets busted in the end. Such was his obsession with "The Mayflower Madam" that Kevin went so far as to actually meet her for dinner while she was on a book tour through Dallas.

It seemed success was going to Kevin's head. Did he really want to be the male Sydney Biddle Barrows? I didn't know but, either way, he was becoming overbearing. The more money we made, the more money he spent.

The suits got more expensive, the jewelry got more flashy, the dinner parties more outrageous. He was trying to make this business legitimate. He was trying to act like a corporate CEO. But as I often had to remind him, we weren't making widgets here, we were selling sex.

And that, we both knew, was illegal…

No matter how you dressed it up, no matter how great your watch was, or how many times you read *The Mayflower Madam*, you had to heed the warning that came at the book's denouement: Sydney Biddle Barrows gets busted in the end.

We'd been lucky so far: flying under the radar of the Dallas vice cops and operating with impunity as we tipped doormen and concierges from one end of the city to the other.

It was almost too good to be true. The men were sweet, handsome, giving, and professional. The nights were pleasant, mild, and we felt no pressure. We had been lulled by good luck and better tips to think that we could do no wrong.

But our luck could only go so far…

We began to disagree and argue more often. I am not sure if I was just growing up and declaring my independence from Kevin or if I was sensing that we were getting too big too soon and, what's worse, attracting too much attention. We were advertising everywhere.

We had too many escorts working for us. Loose lips sink ships, and though Kevin and I were generally discreet you couldn't always trust the "hired help" to be so loyal. It was becoming all-consuming, it wasn't fun anymore. *Kevin* wasn't fun anymore. He was more interested in the thread count of the sheets we were making love on than the act of making love itself.

I usually answered the phones at Kevin's place. I was there a lot, but I kept my apartment, because I still had a lot of stuff and it wouldn't fit in Kevin's place. I was beginning to think *I* didn't fit in anymore, either.

From time to time, Kevin would call me and tell me he "didn't feel well" and he "wanted to be left alone." He would then forward the phones to my house. He would lie in bed for days.

He wouldn't want anyone to see him.

I remember one holiday, when Kevin was sick and I was answering the phones and booking appointments. It was a few days before Christmas when the phone rang, interrupting a marathon wrapping session, not to mention Bing Crosby's *White Christmas*.

I scampered across the living room floor of my apartment, dodging boxes, rolls of gaily patterned wrapping paper, scissors, and tape as I wrapped presents to take home with me to Bridge City, the town of my birth.

The voice on the other end of line was destined to be no grandmother wishing me "Happy Holidays," nor even the sound of my boyfriend, business partner, and mentor Kevin, who was sick and lying low this holiday.

In his stead, he had forwarded the many calls that normally went to his place to come to mine, and thus I was the head phone answerer, chef, and bottle washer answering the phones for what had grown to be a rather large escort service in the metro Dallas area.

Business was booming, thus the small stack of wrapped presents lying pitifully next to the towering mountain of as yet *unwrapped* presents. Needless to say, the sound of ringing phones, and even Bing Crosby, was slowly getting on my already frazzled nerves.

Still, we hadn't become the biggest male escort service in Dallas by letting our emotions get the better of us, and so I was exceedingly polite and businesslike as I answered the phone that cold December day.

It was a new client, calling from his room at the nearby Brookhollow Inn. My jive meter went off instantly; there was just something…*off*…about this particular caller. Answer the phones long enough, and you hear the same things every day. The same buzz words, requests, negotiations, appreciation, expectation. It's enough to school you in what sounds different.

This guy was *definitely* different…

His phrasing was all off; his timing, too. There was something hesitant in his voice, a nervousness that made him sound like the typical homophobic hetero male. Not that we didn't get our share of these "bi-curious" types, but this one sounded angrier than the normal husband stepping out on his wife. In the back of my head was a fateful caveat from Kevin, who had recently warned me that there were a lot of Dallas vice cracking down on male escort services in the area.

I am not sure if it was the underlying hatred of heterosexual males or just pure pride…but I put down my Christmas wrapping paper and took the call personally. Not one to be intimidated, I told the caller that I would be sending a model named "Dolph" to his room.

He agreed and the time was set up to meet at his hotel room. I finished wrapping my presents, showered, made myself presentable, and hit the road. The streets were jammed with last-minute shoppers, every radio station blared carols—more Bing Crosby—and blinking lights could be seen in every passing window, but I felt anything but seasonal cheer.

My boyfriend was "sick," the AIDS crisis was in full bloom, the Dallas vice squad was everywhere, and now I could be showing up to a trap without even wanting to taste the cheese. The appointment was booked for 7 p.m., but I showed up early.

I located the appointed room and listened outside the door, staring down at well-trod carpet and hoping the inhabitants inside couldn't hear my heart pounding through my chest on the other side of the door.

Then again, it would have been hard for them to: I heard many voices inside the room and a porno on Spectra-vision was blaring on the TV. (I assumed, rightfully so, that the taxpayers of Dallas were paying for that little holiday perk.)

Pride, anger, betrayal, and even curiosity forced my only slightly trembling hand to the door as I knocked, forcefully. Everyone inside the room got real quiet, real fast. Finally, a fat bald man opened the door and looked at me with equal parts curiosity and contempt. It was a particularly coy sneer I'd seen one too often in my life, but now it was too late.

I was here.

He was here.

Our destinies were now intertwined.

He was wearing more polyester than a prom king, but looked more appropriate for the part of the aging principal than the vital jock. I noticed a smattering of perspiration dotting his broad, red forehead and smelled the waft of cheap cologne emanating from his coarse, open pores.

I introduced myself as "Dolph" and extended my hand, expecting a firm handshake. What I got was a very insecure, obviously undercover officer telling me to "come inside."

I entered and told him I had to "check in" with the escort service. In reality, I simply called my apartment and talked to the answering machine while I pretended I was talking to a live person. At this point, however, no one even knew where I was. Kevin was too ill to run things personally, and with the holidays upon us we were more short-staffed than usual.

Talk about flying solo…

I was doing this by myself…*for* myself. I was finally facing "the enemy." The undercover officer immediately started trying to get me to agree to sexual favors for money and, when I told him that was not what I did, he became very agitated. His flop sweat multiplied, his cheap cologne turned rancid, and his mood grew equal part superior and sour.

He looked far too old to be a rookie, but his bad acting made me wonder if this was his first day going undercover. He paced in tight circles on the cheap carpet, running a big, beefy hand through his non-existent hair and straining the seams of his polyester pants as he strode past two double-beds with gaudy comforters.

Around this time in Dallas a few cops had been injured in the line of duty, and because I came early they didn't have all the surveillance equipment set up, so the officers in the adjoining rooms could not hear the exchange between the homophobic officer and me.

Far be it from me to give them the time to do so now…

I rushed on, and shortly was in the middle of explaining to him that I was what was known as a "paid companion" and that there was "no sex involved." I quoted him the statue under state law, by memory, a skill that, in addition to fellatio and proper restaurant etiquette, was mandatory for anyone who worked for Kevin, that defines "…money exchanged for sexual favors is considered prostitution and that was a misdemeanor in the state of Texas."

But before I could finish my eloquent speech, six officers burst in the room with their guns drawn and eyes loaded with fear and self-loathing. I was scared. Probably the most scared I'd ever been during my years as a male escort.

There I was at the mercy of seven homophobic, good-ole-boy, pot belly, donut eating cops with guns pointed and eyes blazing. The officer that was pretending—and poorly at that—to be a "client" was pissed off because the other officers had just blown his cover. (I wanted to tell him he'd been doing a fine job of that all by his lonesome, but didn't want to spoil the moment.)

He took the money back from me. He then identified himself as Dallas vice and I was told that the escort service was being investigated for what was known as "Promotion of Prostitution!"

He told me that he "couldn't hold me" but that he would be "vigorously pursuing the agency." (Emphasis on the word *vigorously*.) He added that they would "eventually get a search warrant" and "close down the service."

I waited until I got safely past the six cops with pointed guns and tried to explain that the agency did not "promote prostitution," it was simply "paid companionship." There was no money exchanged for sex at this escort service.

The officer looked at me with wild eyes and shouted, "There is no such thing as paid companionship; it's prostitution. You're a hooker, no matter how you want to look at it. I can't arrest you this time, but we will meet again. I can promise you that. Next time you won't be so lucky!"

I had no reason to doubt him, but didn't stick around to hear anymore. I headed toward the elevator and then for the door, expecting to be busted, clipped, or shot down in a blaze of homophobic bullets by the time I got there.

I was quite shaken when I finally reached my car. I had never experienced anything like that. He called me a hooker. I could have been shot. We were being investigated. It was all spinning through my head.

For the first time it dawned on me that I could go to jail for what I was doing. For what *we* were doing. I could be arrested, locked up, convicted, and shut away for months, maybe even years.

I'd always tried to live a good life, be a good boy, even when my only audience was family members who didn't quite understand me or airline pilots who outright hated me.

Now I was the subject of an investigation; a hooker.

Bah humbug…

The next day I drove home to Bridge City to celebrate Christmas. Despite the inner turmoil that had me tossing and turning the night before, I had to put on a happy face for the family. But amidst the presents and bows and gay wrapping paper, I was preoccupied.

I had to make a decision.

I didn't want to get busted. I didn't want to be branded a HOOKER! That's not who I was; not by a long shot. Hookers were desperate women who walked the street trading sex for drugs, or emaciated young boys fresh from the bus depot hanging out on the street corners in tight jeans and tank tops hoping for a sugar daddy or "chicken hawk" to cruise by in their gleaming Cadillac or BMW.

They weren't…*me.*

When I got back to Dallas just after the holidays, I finally told Kevin what had happened. I just knew he would agree with me. Knew he would be shocked and outraged and paranoid as I'd felt all through the Christmas holiday.

I felt we needed to shut down the agency and get out of Dallas for a while. For whatever reason, though secretly I assumed it was our rapid growth and even Kevin's own grandiose lifestyle a la *The Mayflower Madam*, we had obviously been red-flagged by the cops and were now being investigated.

Shockingly, however, Kevin's reply was a blunt: "We are not promoting prostitution, this is a legitimate business."

I was floored.

"It's not a legitimate business, Kevin," I argued, hardly believing my own ears as I tried to snap him back to reality, cold, hard reality, "these guys are being paid for sex! You are *not* Sydney Biddle Barrows! These good ole boy cops want to bust us and put us in jail! Promotion of prostitution is a felony!"

He wasn't hearing me.

No matter what I said, it was obvious that I wasn't going to convince him. Where was that sultry, sensitive Latin dancer I had fallen in love with? He would have to learn the hard way.

I told him that I was through with the business and that *we* were through, as well. I just couldn't live like this. I felt he was hiding things from me and I wasn't sure if he was even dealing in reality anymore. The suits and the jewelry and the sports cars simply weren't worth it.

To me, the Christmas bust had been a wake-up call, to Kevin it seemed like a mere formality, just one more notch on his rhinestone "pimp belt." I kissed him for the last time and gathered my things and left.

For good…

As I was leaving the phones were ringing, more men searching for hot, anonymous sex. Kevin didn't even follow me to the door to see me out, wish me a fond adieu, instead he just turned and answered the phone and booked a quick appointment.

More money for another new watch…

I realized then that the business had always come first.

No matter what grandiose lies I'd been telling myself, I was obviously second. He had broken his promise. I cried the whole way home. My heart was broken. I felt that I was lost.

Within 48 hours, my entire life had changed.

One day I was a successful escort, making more money than I ever had before and living the good life a cosmopolitan gay male in one of the nation's biggest cities. The next I didn't have a job, I didn't have a boyfriend, and I didn't know where to turn.

I looked in the mirror and I saw this perfect gentleman Kevin had designed. Gone was the small, timid boy from Bridge City, forever hiding his emotions, his needs, his desires. Gone was the brash and impetuous Lance, dancing for dollars and shaking his ass and fantasizing that he was a Chippendale.

Now I saw Dolph Crawford looking back at me!

About six months later, Kevin was busted and charged with "Promotion of Prostitution." (Kevin, I'm sure, was the only one who was surprised at this "shocking" turn of events.) All of his money and cars were seized; he pled guilty and got probation. He left Dallas and moved back home to California.

He died two years later in a charity hospital from complications of AIDS! He died penniless, and I couldn't help but wonder what those final years were like for him. Before he got busted, he had far surpassed his original financial goals for the business. He'd had everything money could buy: clothes, jewelry, cars, good food and wine, WATCHES, tons and tons of watches, but the money had him hooked.

It was his drug.

He never told me he was HIV-positive, but now I know why he was so averse to anal sex and, in a way, I owe him that much: he always made sure we had safe sex. I loved him so much.

His death hit me as a tragic loss and, had I known about his condition, or even his financial straights, I would have surely gotten in touch with him sooner. I thought he was an incredible man, with an incredible vision, doomed only by the trappings of his own success.

In many ways, for better or worse, I credit him for creating Dolph Crawford.

Despite the ugly way it ended, I will never forget him…

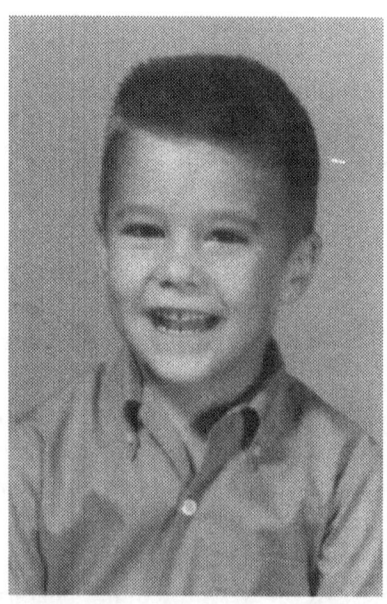

One of my first "professional pictures."
I was so happy and unaware of what was
ahead of me in the 60's, 70's, 80's
and beyond.

So proud of being a scout. The Scouts
taught me to be "proud and obey the law
of the pack." I would later break the law and
be a homosexual. The scouts didn't look kindly on that.

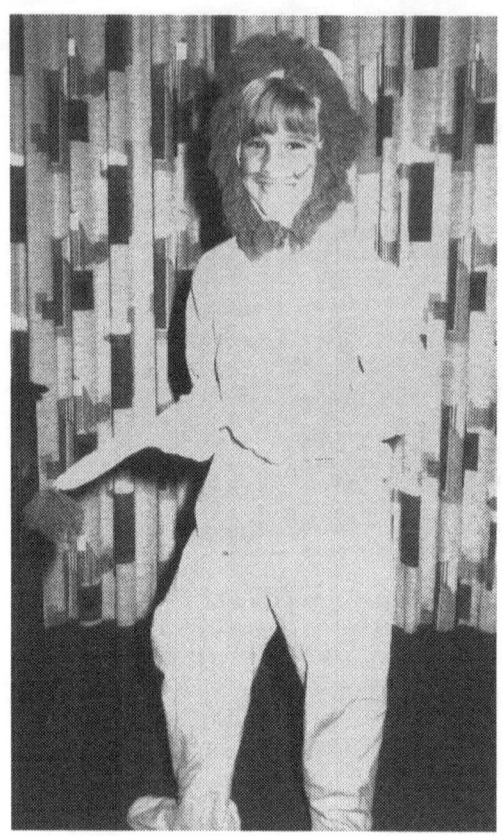

I wanted to be an actor. I loved to perform.
This was a lion costume made by my mom.
I was in my element when I was on stage.
Because I was simply someone else.

I remember taking this picture. It was a perfect day. When
I think of the "child" within me, I always view this picture.
I look so innocent so happy and still so unaware.

I am graduating from high school class of 1981.
I couldn't wait to leave high school. It was
not a positive experience. I couldn't wait to move on.

The "Rainbow Bridge." It was the only way out of my small town. It was a
two-lane bridge. There were only two ways out of my Bridge City: You
either made it across the bridge and into the world or you jumped to
your death. I mourn for the souls that jumped.

A full length picture of "Lance." My gay version
of a Chippendale dancer. I grew out the hair
and really hit the weights.

"Lance" making a double bicep poise. I had been dancing about a year.
I was content that I could dance and make a living and support myself.

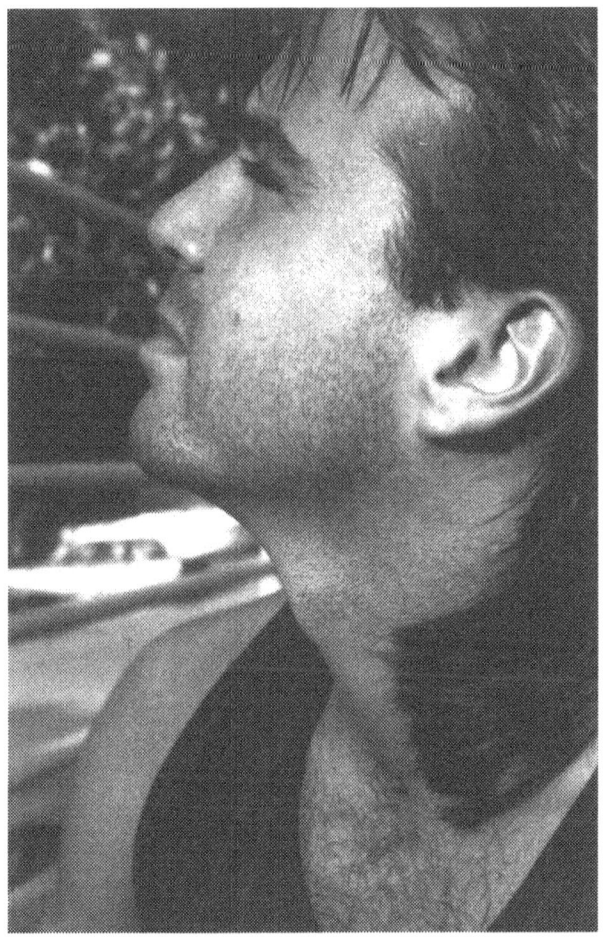

More of "Lance" looking forward.
Wondering what comes next.

This is a photo I did while I was escorting with Kevin.
It sums up how I was feeling.
I had made the transformation from dancing to escorting.
This photo would be used in a line of greeting cards
by photographer Rolf Juario.
The card that it covered for was a symathy card.
I thought that was appropriate.

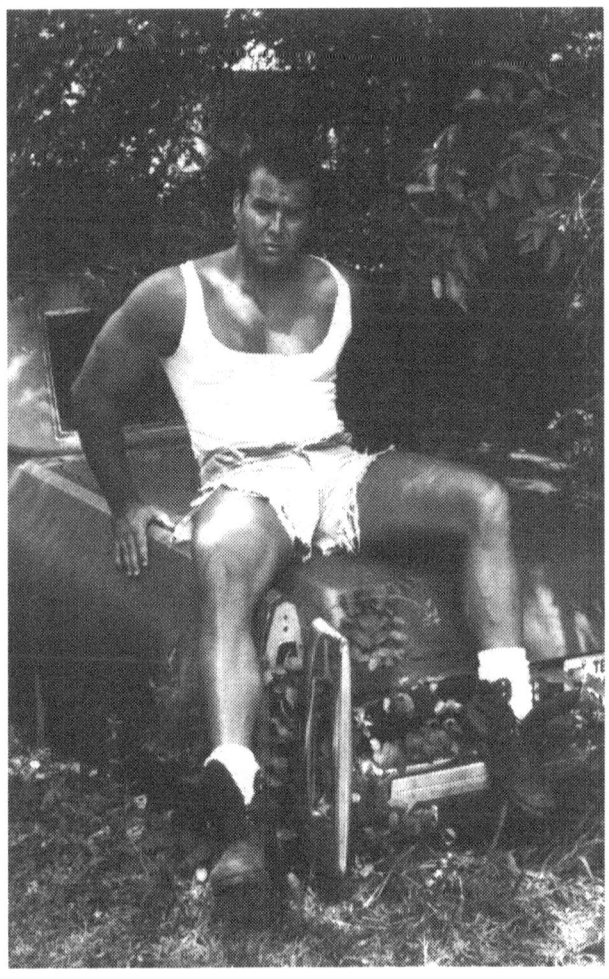

Here's Dolph Crawford. This photo was shot by
photographer James Franklin. Brought out the "white trash" side.
But remember: White trash don't burn.

Another Dolph Shot. More muscular, more cocky. Less afraid. More confident. Finally Dolph thinks he has everything he wants. A great partner and a thriving business. Photograph by James Franklin.

I thought this picture captured the hard,
tough guy that Dolph had become.
The person that life had made cold.
The big chest protects his vulnerable heart.
The muscles keep the homophobic male at bay. It's all an illusion.

I graduated from Massage School. I am holding my state
license in my hand. I would keep that license for 15 years.
Until the state of Texas took it away from me in 2002. I can't
write about how they were able to do that, because they have
gagged my right to Freedom of Speech.

I met Cher in 1981. I was so impressed with her.
She was very nice and offered to pose for a picture.
We both looked so different then and have changed a lot over the years.
I still admire Cher to this day. She is a survivor.

Dolph body shot. 5'10" 215 lbs of natural muscle.

Most recent pictures of Dolph. At the beach. Near the ocean.
The place where Dolph feels free.

Dolph at 40 at the beach.
The salt water is very cleansing.

Although Dolph has been gagged by the state of Texas,
he still looks toward the future.
He still believes he can make a difference.
He can use his life to evoke change.
He is centered and he is very aware of finally who he is and what his
purpose in life will be.

Dolph continues on his journey. Still battling obstacles, but more secure and knowledgeable about life. Armed with the "Secrets and Lies" the state of Texas never wants YOU the public to know.

6

The Vivid Years

After I left the escort agency, I was on my own again.

I had made enough money to pay my bills for a while, but I knew it wouldn't last and that I would have to reinvent myself yet again. I felt like one of those chameleons you always see on the Discovery Channel, forever changing his color to blend into his environment.

In Bridge City I played the straight man, literally. In the air, I was the happy-go-lucky male flight attendant, non-threatening to those future G. I. Joe's and friend to stewardesses everywhere.

On the stage I was Lance, the super-buffed Chippendale dancer, fulfilling every man's desire with his bulging thong and rippling muscles. As an escort, I'd been the "perfect gentleman" Kevin had designed me to be, wining and dining my clients into homo heaven seven nights a week.

Who would I be next?

I was so depressed and lost without Kevin. I traveled around from club to club and danced to make extra money. I felt as if I was just existing; running just to stand still. Shaking my ass, doing the bump and grind, just like I'd always tried to avoid, but gone was the passion I'd once had for my audience.

Gone was the illusion of Lance. Now Dolph stared back, too wise, too sad, too good for those scarred stages. Despite the sadness and ennui, I still didn't drink, still didn't do drugs.

I just slept a lot, worked out, and danced part-time. I felt I was just going through the motions, waiting to arrive in my next environment so I could change my true colors once again.

One night while dancing at a Dallas nightclub, I ran into a good friend I had met earlier in my dancing career, an older man in his fifties named Ted. Ted had gray hair and a salt and pepper beard to match. He looked like your typical community college math teacher, but his wise eyes belied a kind, gentle man.

He was always compassionate to me in the bars. He knew what had happened with Kevin and understood that I needed to put that whole scene behind me. To that end, he approached me with a proposition that night.

He told me that he was starting a "production company." When I looked at him quizzically, wondering what he was going to "produce," he explained that he was going to be making "adult gay movies."

He had camera and editing experience, he explained, he just needed good looking young male models that could read lines and take direction and perform sex in front of a camera.

He wanted me to be one of his models.

Well, I immediately shot down *that* idea. I told Ted that I was not going to do *any* movies. When he asked why, I explained adamantly that I didn't want my "sex life caught on film."

After all, I had big dreams for my future and I wasn't going to have some porn movie ruin the legitimate life I dreamed of having one day. He was disappointed, at first, but quickly shrugged it off.

He asked me if I could help him "cast" the films since I knew a lot of dancers and escorts in the Dallas area. Suddenly, Kevin's business acumen took over and I told him that I would cast his movies only if he would make me a full partner in the production company.

As Ted hemmed and hawed, I perfected my pitch: He could teach me all he knew about camera, lighting, and editing. Show me the ropes. I could assist him in directing. We could work together and make it a big success. Ted finally agreed and we combined our talents and created Trac Productions.

Turns out, Trac was exactly what I needed at just the right time. I was determined to stay busy until I got through this heart broken-depression over Kevin. Starting a new business venture with an old friend was just what I needed.

Ted told me what type of models he wanted and I searched for them diligently. It wasn't hard; despite what its county commissioners might have thought, Dallas had a thriving gay scene and sexy male models were everywhere I turned.

I was like a modeling agent.

I would interview the prospective models, take Polaroid pictures of them, along with some vital stats, and then Ted and I would sift through the pictures to choose who we thought best fit whatever particular role we were trying to cast. We would both make a decision of the final models for the movie. We needed four strong models for the first feature.

It turns out that Ted and I worked well together. We each brought something unique and special to the project, and it was refreshing being appreciated for my brain for once, instead of just my body. It was hard work writing scripts, blocking scenes, scouting for locations, finding models, casting models, but it was rewarding, too. It kept me very busy.

But I needed busy in my life…

We really lucked out, because as good fortune would have it just as we were launching Trac Productions, Vivid Video was also making the crossover into the lucrative gay adult film market. Suddenly, Vivid was looking to get its hands on new films and they had money to spend on them.

Lots of money…

Vivid was a powerhouse in the adult film industry, not just because of their beautiful stars and slick production values, but mostly due to their innovative approach to treating the porn industry as a legitimate business.

Far from hiding out in back alleys and cheap hotel rooms, they were the first adult film business that really put money into the box covers for their videos. Vivid hired a high fashion photographer in California and spent big bucks on making the box cover shot look "Hollywood." As a result, it would really catch the customer's eye. The box cover, Vivid knew, was the big sell.

Thanks to our great timing and the hard work we'd put into planning our first feature, Ted made a deal with Vivid for one movie. He pitched them the script and showed them the Polaroids of the models we chose and, amazingly, Vivid bought it. Suddenly, we were in business!

Things happened quickly after that; within weeks the contractual details and final deals were all finalized and we were a legitimate production company with our very first client. Vivid wanted the first movie wrapped in a month. Vivid executives fronted us the expense money and agreed to pay the other half on delivery of the film.

Now the real work began: Ted and I made an agreement with a local camera company to lease the cameras and lighting and editing equipment we would need to create a video worthy of Vivid's high production values.

To save money, we finagled a deal where we would pay a one-day rate and they would allow us to pick up the equipment at the end of the business day on Friday and return it first thing Monday morning.

Kind of like a three-for-one deal…

(Hmmm, that sounds like the title of a good gay porn video!)

Despite the craftiness of our slick wrangling, this still meant we only had one weekend to shoot the movie and then we would edit the following weekend.

For this breakneck pace to work out, obviously, things had to run smoothly. We both knew that we would only get one chance to make a good impression with a powerhouse company like Vivid. If we turned in shoddy work or made excuses on this first opportunity, there would likely be no second.

The models were hired, the location was prepared, and the equipment was set up and ready to shoot. The first movie we would make was called *4 x 4*. Ted wrote it and I thought it was a great idea.

I hired the four models, making sure they were compatible sexually. There would be 2 bottoms, 2 tops, etc., and it was vital for this first video that the models were comfortable with not just their roles, but their partners as well.

I was in charge of the models, so I instructed all four of them to arrive at the location at 6 a.m. that Saturday morning. When 6 a.m. rolled around, however, I arrived at the location and found only three models waiting to perform. My fourth model was nowhere to be found!

I called his house and his pager…no answer!

I kept thinking he would walk in any minute…he didn't!

Ted was growing worried…I was growing furious…the other three models were growing impatient and anxious. I thought I could trust this model. I made it clear that they were not to work the night before, get to bed early, and be on time!

I felt like a den mother at a frat house…

Make that *Animal House*.

Ted finally pulled me aside and said, "Listen Dolph, we need four guys for this video to work."

"I know," I said grimly. Then I suggested we "shoot around the scene" until the fourth model finally showed up.

"He's not showing, Dolph," Ted replied, growing frantic. "It's 10 a.m. If he was going to show up, he would have been here hours ago. We're wasting time."

Trying to be reasonable, I suggested we change the script and call it *3 x 3*. It seemed like a plausible solution to me.

Ted responded, "No, Dolph, we can't just switch gears in mid-stream. Vivid approved a script called *4 x 4*; we have to shoot 4 models!"

Now I was the one who was frantic!

"I know Ted," I said. "What do you want me to do? We can't waste this shooting day."

Ted quietly suggested something that hadn't even entered my mind: "Dolph, you must be the fourth model."

"What!" I responded, shocked. "No way. I am *not* going to be in a porno, Ted. We talked about his before!"

Ted replied more calmly this time. His decision had obviously been made, now he was simply proving his case to his reluctant business partner. "Need I remind you that you were in charge of the casting, Dolph? You were told to provide four models. You only have three. You're a partner in this company and, therefore, you must step up and be the fourth model. I'm sorry, Dolph, I just don't see any other way for this to work."

Damn!

But even as I fought the notion, I had to admit that he was right. It was the only solution. As badly as I didn't want to admit it, I knew I had no other choice; we had already wasted three precious, not to mention *expensive*, hours waiting for the missing model.

We still had at least two days of shooting ahead of us. We only had the equipment and the models paid for two days of shooting. I had no other choice; I had made a commitment to Ted, he trusted me enough to make me partner in Trac Productions. I couldn't let him down now.

I would have to make the movie and be in front of the camera. I was not happy, to say the least, but I was professional and put on a good face. I didn't want the other models to think this was beneath me.

Surprisingly, it went rather smoothly. Once shooting began, the scenes were shot one by one. It may look erotic and sexually charged on screen, and the filming had its moments, but most of what we did that day was a technical exercise in angles, lighting, and careful choreography.

To his credit, they were all locked perfectly and directed beautifully by Ted. He was great at making models feel comfortable and communicating and directing each scene to illicit the best performance, both sexual and artistic, from his models.

It was hard for me to concentrate on acting; the whole time I was watching the monitors and checking the camera angles and double-checking the lighting. The lights were hot. It was difficult to perform.

I hated being in front of the camera, but once I saw the finished product I was relieved that my hesitance never showed on film. Despite a rough beginning, the shooting wrapped on schedule.

Ted was happy and appreciated that I had stepped up to the plate and was responsible as not just a friend, but a business partner. Although no one else knew, Ted knew that I didn't want to be on film.

His deep sense of appreciation meant a lot to me…

The following weekend we edited *4 x 4*. Though I had made a living off of my body for the last few years, I hated seeing myself on camera. As a result, I made Ted teach me how to edit. The minute he did, I tried to edit myself out of the film as much as I could.

I never left a shot that showed my face in a full on, up front shot. Ted understood and, surprisingly, complied. We were both exhausted from the breakneck pace, but I noticed that Ted would lie down and nap frequently while we took breaks or even when I was editing.

I just thought it was because he was older and needed more rest.

We finished editing and delivered the master copy to Vivid. On time, and with four models instead of three. We sweated their reaction, but were pleasantly surprised when, without a hitch, the execs at Vivid sent us the rest of our money as scheduled. Two weeks later, Ted met with me and told me that Vivid had liked the film *4 x 4*!

His face grew serious as he told me that he had "good news and bad news." Ever the optimist, I told him to tell me the good news first. He replied that Vivid was so impressed with the movie they wanted to do an eight picture deal with us over one year! I was ecstatic!

"Eight pictures, that is some great money," I thought, then said out loud, "That's fabulous news, Ted. What could possibly be the bad news?"

"Well, they had one stipulation," Ted remarked. "They want Dolph Crawford in all eight movies."

"Hell no!" I thought. "No way. I was not doing anymore films. I stepped up once and I am not stepping up again." I ranted to Ted for about 10 minutes, going on and on about my legitimate career and dreams for the future and self-respect.

Ted listened, then patiently explained the harsh realities of the video porn industry, "I told them all that, Dolph, but they saw you as a lead actor. They think you can carry the movies and the only way they would do an eight picture deal is with *you* as a lead actor. It would lend name recognition to each film and establish Dolph Crawford as a legitimate porn star."

"No!" I shouted, unwilling and, in fact, unable to consider that possibility for myself. Already just being on *one* porn video was making me a paranoid wreck, with nightmares about my family and friends finding out and shaming me for life. Eight would be a death sentence for sure.

"I don't want that reputation, Ted," I insisted to my friend and business partner. "I have had enough of a past, especially for a twenty-five-year-old. I am going legitimate! I won't compromise my life again!"

When I finally stopped yelling, I noticed that Ted was crying. I was disappointed, too. After all, that was a lot of money Vivid was offering, but it wasn't worth crying over. Or so I thought.

I finally asked Ted why he was crying. He told me that "he couldn't talk about it" and simply continued to weep.

I explained to him that I wanted Trac Productions to succeed, but I couldn't compromise my standards again…I just wouldn't.

He informed me that he wasn't crying about that.

"I have something I have to tell you, Dolph," he said as he looked up at me with tears running down his kind, gentle face. "I have full blown AIDS! I don't have any health insurance and I can't afford the medications I need to stay healthy and fight off the virus. I need this money so that I can get the proper health care. If I lose this contract with Vivid, I lose everything."

I was speechless.

My heart broke for Ted. He was a very private, very proud man. It took a lot for him to tell me that. I knew then that the situation was desperate. No way would a proud man like Ted reveal his deepest, darkest secret if the situation wasn't indeed dire.

I asked him how long he had.

He told me that his "T-cell count was very low" and without proper medical care he had only "about five months, max."

I remember feeling bad about ranting and raving in front of Ted. He was so good to me. He was dealing with life and death issues, literally, and I was standing there acting all self-righteous and bitching about having my face on camera with one of the most well-respected and successful companies in the porn business.

I made a decision that very moment. I looked at Ted and told him that he wasn't going to die and that we were going to be partners in Trac Productions for a very, *very* long time.

I hugged him and he wept in my arms and thanked me countless times. The unstated message was clear that day: He was counting on me and I couldn't let him down. Ted needed me and, frankly, I needed to be needed.

Despite my trepidation, both professional and personal, I signed the contract for eight films with Vivid. Once again circumstances put me in a position I didn't want to be in and, despite my better judgment, I gave in.

Unfortunately, it wouldn't be the last time…

For the next few weeks, we were busier than ever.

We took two full months to write scripts and cast models for all eight films. The way we figured it, if we wrote the script and sketched out the storyboards and cast the models first, for all eight videos, the shoots themselves would go much more smoothly than starting right away and figuring everything out as we went along.

We were right…

Ever the visionary, Ted wanted to draft a plan to make each movie different and perhaps even do a series of three films, a trilogy. (*Lord of the Rings*, eat your heart out!) He felt the last three movies should be a trio of films with a local flavor, something like a "Texas Tales" series.

He thought that we should have enough experience by that time to master an outdoor location shoot to give the trilogy some real pizzazz. I agreed. We still had to scout out the locations, make arrangements with camera crews, and decide on which models we would use for each film.

I had learned my lesson the first time.

For future films, I would be casting an alternate model for just such an emergency in case there was a "no show" model. If we didn't use the alternate model in front of the camera, I reasoned, we would utilize him behind the camera. There was always a need for an extra hand, either holding a boom mike or adjusting lighting or simply hauling that crate and toting that bail.

Finally, our shooting schedule was set. The models were confirmed and now it was time to start cranking out the movies. The comparison wasn't far off, for that's exactly what we did: crank them out.

Hard to Hold was the next film we did for Vivid on our eight-picture deal. Then we did a movie called *Hot Property*. Then we shot a featured called, appropriately enough, *Three the Hard Way*. The movies were running smoothly and, after a few months, we were right on schedule.

Not surprisingly, the models enjoyed the money but what surprised me most was that they *all* wanted to be selected for the box cover shoot. Although I tried to tell them that once they were on the box cover anyone who walked into the video store would see them on the cover, they couldn't have cared less; they all wanted to be selected for the cover.

Since I was never one to disappoint anyone, I was relieved that, ultimately, the selection was not in Trac Production's control; the executives at Vivid would pick the cover models themselves.

They would fly the selected models to Los Angeles, all expenses paid, and they would arrange for the models to then be shot by a high fashion photographer who, in the best Vivid style, would make them look fabulous.

The models would also be paid extra for the cover shoot, but I knew that wasn't why our boys wanted to be cover material. Despite the fact that I knew Vivid was trying to build a porn star around the name Dolph Crawford, I was firm about not wanting to be on anymore box covers. I was only on one cover, and that was the first one: *4 x 4*. That was the only one I agreed to.

Surprisingly, the execs at Vivid complied with my wishes…

Each film was rigorous for me personally, as the pressure was really on for me to act in, help direct, and then work the cameras when I wasn't in a scene. As a result, I was exceedingly busy.

Even though our budgets were getting increasingly bigger, we still kept the original scenario: We'd rent the equipment for one weekend, paying only the one-day fee, and the editing was always done the following weekend in one long, marathon session.

Meanwhile, Ted was getting steadily weaker. I was having to do more of the editing work, even as he lay behind me on a couch dozing in and out of sleep. With our first three films of the contract in the can, I didn't even know if he would be able to make five more films, let alone live to see his prized trilogy make it to the small screen. He seemed to get tired more frequently now, and even when he was up and around he seemed exceedingly weak and fragile.

He never complained and always did his job well, but when I saw he was weakening I would always somehow manage to cover for him. The models never suspected a thing and, fortunately, the big wigs back at Vivid had no idea. We never talked about his illness again; he asked me not to discuss it with anyone. I agreed, and Trac Productions kept shooting.

One day in between movies I was relaxing by the pool at my apartment. It was there that I first met a guy named Jim. He was obviously gay and had heard through the local "gay grapevine" that I was casting "adult movies."

He was intrigued, like most people are, about the behind the scenes antics in shooting adult movies. I explained to him it was not all that glamorous.

"The lights are hot," I described, "it's not very sexy, you have to be very mechanical sexually. It's almost like math, or putting together a bike on Christmas morning: Slot A goes into Tab B, but look over here and lift your leg a bit higher, no, not that leg, the other leg.

"You have to get in certain positions, allow for the right camera angle, it's really quite technical. And most importantly, you have to give the director notice when you were ready for the 'money shot'—the climax shot—this shot was very important and had to be captured perfectly. Everything hinged around the money shot."

Jim seemed interested, but also somewhat prudish.

"I could never do an adult movie," he insisted, as if what I did for a living was beneath him, "it would ruin my reputation in Dallas."

"Well," I agreed somewhat cynically, the hot Texas sun beating down on us both as we sat there talking about gay porn in the middle of the day, "unfortunately, I have already ruined mine."

The sarcastic comment was not that far from the truth. By now the movies we'd done previously had hit the video stores and people in Dallas were watching them and actually recognizing me.

What's more, I was seen in male magazines on newsstands all over the country and my still photos from the movies—particularly the money shots—were marketed in every gay magazine to further publicize, and hopefully sell, the movie. I had no control over that…it was Vivid's property now.

Sometimes, it felt like *I* was their property, too…

The models who I had previously warned about doing the box covers were now angry at me because, just as I predicted, they were noticed on box covers and now it affected their lives and relationships in a negative way.

A lot of these models were guys with professional jobs and some were in committed relationships that they truly valued. Being on the box cover of a gay adult video wasn't exactly helping their cache in the "real world."

You couldn't miss a Vivid box cover; they were done so well and so professionally. They stuck out amongst the other trashy looking covers in the video store, with their 70s feel and bad lighting, immediately drawing the eye and giving the cover models something they at first wanted, and then scorned: instant recognition.

Vivid had mastered the art of box covers; as a result they made Vivid's movies *very* popular. But my former models were very miserable. Sometimes I couldn't understand it; it's like they thought the movies would never be released.

But they were…and quickly, I might add. Usually two months after we wrapped a movie, Vivid already had it on the adult bookstore shelves. They were determined to flood the gay market.

And that's exactly what they did.

Vivid were the undisputed leaders at distribution and marketing. The movies were everywhere and selling and renting in major numbers. But Vivid didn't just excel at speed, their commitment to quality added to their longevity as well: Almost twenty years later, most of my movies are still on the video shelves.

A few days after first meeting Jim I was at the pool again going over video scripts and details getting ready to cast the next film, called *Men TV*. Not surprisingly, Jim wandered out to the pool again. This time, however, he wasn't alone; he brought a very good looking, blonde haired, blue eyed" buddy" with him. He introduced himself as Pierce.

For my part, I was immediately taken with Pierce.

He was very nice looking: tall, built, and very handsome in an "innocent" sort of way. Some of the men I tended to socialize in the nightclubs and especially gay clubs eventually grew a hard, rough edge to them. Comparatively speaking, Pierce was like a cherub.

A cherub in a thong, that is…

I could tell that Pierce was interested in me as well, because he immediately made it clear he and Jim were "just friends." The body language was subtle, the words he used clear, and in that searing Texas sunlight the ingredients of our chemical attraction began oozing into a fine, thin crust.

I could sense that Jim, on the other hand, would have liked his relationship with Pierce to be much more than friendship. But Pierce was definitely letting me know he was available.

As for myself, I was definitely interested.

I hadn't dated since Kevin. Not seriously, anyway. It was just too difficult for me. I didn't want to get hurt again. Most of the guys I met, perhaps merely because of the business I was in, were all about results: What could I do for them? What could we do for each other? What could they get out of our relationship that might further their careers along?

As we talked that fateful day, I could tell that Jim was obviously sensing an attraction between Pierce and me. As a result, he announced to Pierce in a very condescending way that I was casting porn movies, and jokingly suggested Pierce "should interview" with me.

For his part, Jim laughed at his mean-spirited suggestion. Pierce and I didn't. Pierce kindly asked me for a piece of paper and pen and quickly scribbled down his number.

"I would really be interested in learning more about what you do, Dolph" he said seriously, sincerely, and much to Jim's obvious chagrin, "and learning more about *you* in the process."

I was speechless.

It had been a long time since someone made me blush, let alone made me excited. Pierce was doing all that, and then some. I took his number and quickly excused myself from the pool.

My swimsuit was all of a sudden getting very…*tight*.

I couldn't wait to call Pierce.

I hadn't been this excited about dating someone in a long time, and the rush of adrenaline and expectation was a welcome change from the daily grind of writing, casting, shooting, and acting in the Vivid videos.

Pierce was not the typical guy that I dated. He was not older than I was, instead he was closer to my age. He was not rugged, which was another attribute I often sought out. Instead, he was more gentle and sweet.

He didn't seem too controlling, either, which was a pleasant change from dominating boyfriends like Kevin had been. He seemed to look right through the tan, buffed-out character Dolph and see me lurking inside. My mind was racing with expectation!

The very next night I called him.

I was currently casting for *Men TV*, and to assuage my nervousness, that's what I made sure the initial conversation was based around. A business call, nothing more. He seemed as if he was genuinely interested in being in the movie, so I kept the conversation about casting, and what we were looking for, and how much we paid, etc.

Despite his eagerness, and obvious good looks, I had mixed feelings about casting Pierce for the movie. I wasn't sure I wanted him in that part of my life. A part that even *I* didn't want to be in. I wanted him to get to know *me* first, outside of business, outside of the harsh lighting and strict angles and sexual geometry.

I wanted him to get to know me outside of porn.

I wanted it to be a great love affair, not just another business venture like it had been with Kevin. In that relationship, as I had learned so cruelly, business had come first, emotions second.

After all the tough breaks in my life, I was still a hopeless romantic. I wanted the fairy tale love affair to come true. I could easily see him being my mate. It was just an instant connection that day by the pool and then, on the phone, we talked so easily I just felt…comfortable.

We met the next night after he got off work. It was supposed to be a casual get together. "Stop by and we'll talk about the script," I'd offered in my best "talent scout" voice, trying to sound achingly casual.

He came over in a tight T-shirt and ripped jeans.

Even in the casual garb, Pierce was truly a sight to behold: He had the tightest body and the greatest ass I had ever seen. (And by now, I'd pretty much seen them all!) We talked for a while and then it was time to get down to business.

Literally…

After he filled out all the paperwork for Trac Productions, "sign here, sign there," I had to take the standard Polaroids on which we based the model selection. Tentatively at first, he got undressed and posed in different positions for the camera. Suddenly the walls closed in, it seemed like all the air left the room.

My sole focus became this naked creature posing seductively in my foggy viewfinder. The camera, then my eyes, sought out every nook and cranny of his sumptuous young body. The outline of his ribs against firm, tan flesh. The arc of his calves, the swell of his thighs.

I was so turned on by what I was seeing, my hands were quickly growing moist on the big, clunky Polaroid camera. For the first time I felt like a voyeur, looking at a delicate young creature through the fish-eye camera lens as I imagined myself partaking of all the earthly pleasures his heavenly body promised.

It almost seemed too good to be true that this fiery young morsel was standing there in my living room, offering himself up to the Polaroid camera. To me. The pictures that spat out and slowly developed definitely didn't do him justice: In person, he was much sexier.

I tried to tell him so, to assuage his nervousness. He seemed at once equal parts proud and embarrassed. He seemed to be crossing some imaginary line he'd drawn for himself in the sand.

"In for a penny, in for a pound," I could almost hear him murmur.

After we took the pictures, I could see that he was fully aroused. If I'd been directing the scene for a porno, let's call it *His First Porn Audition*, this would be the moment when I'd call out, "Action!" and start filming.

Instead I put the camera down and thickly told him he could "get dressed." I tried to stay professional. Tried to stay in control of the situation, though every pore of my body ached with longing. In all this time I had never had sex with any of the models I had hired, *off* camera that is.

I felt that it blurred the lines of "professionalism."

If that even existed in the porn industry, that is.

I turned back around after putting the camera down and Pierce was still standing there, naked. Inviting. Aroused. His smooth tight body, so hard and so lean, so tan and so young, waited there invitingly for me. His abs rippled with muscle, his legs and ass were sculpted like a Greek statue, he was like the answer to a dream come true.

"Do you really want me to get dressed?" he asked in a voice at once both awkward and commanding. I didn't reply. I didn't need to. We both knew the answer. For once I cast my professionalism aside and walked across the room and grabbed him and kissed him passionately. (He was a great kisser.) I then took him to the bedroom and we had the best sex that I had ever had.

Yes, I said it: The best sex I'd ever had, hands down. (Or up, depending on the sexual position!) I was a pro in the escort business, I had been promiscuous in my early twenties, and by now had four porno videos under my belt.

But nothing compared to this night of unfettered, raw sex...

He was the perfect lover, a flickering angel suspended in time, at once fiery and dominating, and then just as quickly aching and submissive. I couldn't find a single flaw. He was exactly what I was looking for. And apparently he felt the same way, because that night, after hours of passionate sex, he asked if he could stay and I heard myself quickly answer, "Yes!"

Pierce never left.

He moved in the next week and we slept together every night. We had sex constantly, at least three times a day. I never got tired of his body. I never grew tired of his face. There was always some new angle to view him in, always some new position to try. He was energetic and free, always willing to try something to new.

To learn.

To teach...

I longed for him to hurry and get home from work every day. For once, I let him get close to me. Not just the outside, the physical gifts we exchanged, again and again and again, but inside as well, deep down to my throbbing, aching heart.

I gave him my body and my soul, a first for me. He did the same for me. I just knew that I had finally found the man that I would spend the rest of my life with. I felt alive again.

With *Men-TV* in pre-production, and despite my ardent warnings, Pierce still felt that he wanted to be a part of what I was doing. He wanted to be in the film. I wasn't keen on the idea, but it was too early in our relationship for me to be pushy and tell him, flat out, "No, it's not a good idea."

Instead, I told him all the negative things about the video business. I told him it would be on every shelf of every adult bookstore in the country, mere months after we shot it. Once the film was handed over to Vivid, I warned, they owned it and all its contents.

They could re-edit and make various "Best of" videos (which they did with most of my movies). They could release his pictures to any magazine or gay newspaper around the country, and even around the world. Once he did a movie for Vivid, he would be a public figure in the gay community.

The technology was rapidly advancing, I warned him.

Every month, it seemed, the powers that be in the porn industry, both gay and straight, found some new way to exploit those that made adult movies. The images, so naked and stark, were sold and re-sold again and again, popping up who knows where. Ads for phone sex lines.

For escort services.

As layouts in adult magazines.

I gave it to him straight. He listened, patiently, and then he told me he still wanted to be in the movie, *Men-TV*.

When I showed him Pierce's Polaroids and told him I'd found the co-star of our next video, Ted was ecstatic. (He even had the perfect screen name for him: "Pierce Mathews." Get it? Pierce?)

As for myself, I kept my opinions private. I didn't like it. I just knew that nothing good would come from this. But it's what he wanted and he had already given me so much in the few short weeks we'd known each other, I would always give him what he wanted.

We started shooting *Men-TV* on a Saturday and by now we had such a system down, it truly ran smooth and perfectly. System or no system, this shoot was different from all the rest: I didn't like seeing my boyfriend on film.

I didn't like seeing other men touching him.

Giving him pleasure. Receiving pleasure from him. Sweating. Writhing. Groping. I was jealous. I didn't show it, but I wanted to get this movie wrapped and in the can as quickly as possible. My only hope as we finally finished shooting late that next day was that Pierce wouldn't want to do anymore.

Little did I know how futile that hope would be...

The hits just kept on coming: Once the movie was finished, I got word from Ted that Vivid wanted "Pierce Mathews" for the cover. By himself. I wasn't surprised. I knew they would like him.

After all, I loved him.

Why wouldn't they?

But this was the first time they had ever asked for just *one* model for the video box cover. To me, that spoke volumes about Pierce and his potential to go far in this business. A business I wanted him to steer clear of.

After I got the news from Ted, I immediately gave Pierce my same speech about the box cover exposure. Regardless, he seemed fine with it. He *wanted* to do it. He wanted to make the extra money. He wanted to fly to LA and be shot by a fashion photographer.

My jealousy grew stronger.

But I managed it. I quietly booked the flight and even put him on the plane. The cover turned out great: everyone was happy. Vivid loved Pierce and saw him as a lead actor. Ted was also happy because this meant that we now had *two* major porn stars associated with our production company: First Dolph Crawford and now the new kid on the block, Pierce Mathews.

For his part, Pierce loved the shoot and enjoyed all the attention. I could see him getting sucked in by the lifestyle. The easy answers, the giving fans, the adoring public, the view from the top.

It seemed as if I was the only one that wanted to finish the rest of these eight films and take my boyfriend away from this whole crazy porn world. After his cover and video debuted, Pierce did photo layouts and got other contract offers. I didn't want to hear about them.

I didn't want to know about them.

My jealousy was getting the best of me, both personally and professionally. I had so wanted to shield Pierce from the business end of porn, to keep him from becoming a household name in this industry, to keep that angelic face, shy smile, and awkward boyishness from getting hard, slick, and glossy.

Part of it was selfish, I admit. I wanted Pierce all to myself. That face. That body. That heart. That soul. They were mine, all mine. Weren't they? But also I wanted to protect Pierce and his future.

He was young, naive, and impressionable. What did he know? I'd seen it happen all too often: that awe-shucks naiveté taken advantage of and sucked out of him. And now all my predictions had come true. Now that thing which I so desired to covet for myself was public property, and in a big way.

As a result, I poured myself back into work getting ready for the next movie. Pierce and I were apart a lot because now I had to travel and scout out our next location. I finally found it in Oklahoma.

It was a huge, 600-acre ranch right on the water. It was very private, secluded, and hidden away from the prying eyes of the other townspeople. This, it was decided, was where we would shoot Ted's long-awaited *Texas Tales* series.

Ted and I planned to shoot the entire series over a week. Then we would edit it down to three separate series movies. After that, we would finally have fulfilled our lucrative eight movie contract with Vivid.

I, for one, was more than ready to get it done, over with. Meanwhile, Pierce was busy traveling, doing photo shoots and magazine layouts and enjoying the heady rush of fan adulation.

I was traveling, too, but in opposite directions while promoting *my* former movies for Vivid. Basically, I was showing up at video stores and signing box covers. Signing autographs for men both black and white, rich and poor, tall and short, thin and fat, fabulously desirable and dull as dirt.

It didn't matter to me anymore.

I didn't know them and they didn't know me, although they *thought* they did. By now Dolph Crawford had become a star. Not the star I wanted to be, known for my inner thoughts, desires, talents, creativity, and emotions, but a star in the same right. The promotional whizzes at Vivid had done their job well, and now I was what they had created me to be: a gay porn star.

For this shoot, we packed up the entire cast and crew and headed to Madill, Oklahoma. Picture it: Here we are driving into this small town with crew trucks, large camera equipment, and fifteen gay porn models decked out in tight tank tops, skimpy cut-off jeans, and hiking boots. No matter how hard we tried to keep things "low key," it turns out this little Okie town would never forget us.

For their part, the townspeople were very friendly and curious.

When we would go into town to eat or shop, it was like the circus had come to town. As a result, we mostly stayed on the ranch where we were shooting. There was a large house there, plenty of room for us to stretch out and explore, and it was just easier that way.

The days, like the videos themselves, were hot, steamy, and long. We were shooting outside for the first time. Not surprisingly, we ran into many obstacles along the way. We had to shoot early to get the right sunlight and we had to shoot at dawn, too. It made for long days.

And sex-charged nights….

The models loved it, but, as head model wrangler, I had to keep them from hooking up at night. Hard as it was, I made them save it for the camera. They were like my children.

I was bossier than ever.

Somehow, it worked.

Meanwhile, Pierce was on my mind more than ever as he did the "star thing" back home. I wondered what he was doing. Worse, I wondered *who* he was doing it with. I wondered if he missed me.

I know I missed him.

I couldn't wait to finish these three movies and go home to Dallas and take a trip with my boyfriend somewhere secluded and safe and finally put this porn business behind us, once and for all.

My only salvation was that at least Pierce had been too busy off doing his own thing to star in the *Texas Tales* videos; I'm not sure the green-eyed monster of jealousy that held me prisoner could have taken it!

I was exhausted every day.

The shoots were long. And hard on me, personally, now more than ever. Ted was just not able to work as much anymore. He mostly just directed, watching the monitors from a director's chair and making suggestions that weren't always on target.

I didn't blame him. Far from it. His energy was gone, sucked dry from the disease that was ravaging his body. He tried his best, but I could see that the virus was taking its toll.

We finally wrapped the *Texas Tales Series*. Still, the models wanted to spend another night in the rambling ranch house that had become our home away from home for lo these past few weeks.

Despite their enthusiasm, I strongly objected. I just wanted to get home. I had called home several times and Pierce wasn't answering. Naturally, I felt something might be wrong.

Furthermore, I knew that Ted wasn't feeling well. He needed to get home as well. So we loaded the trucks and said goodbye to Madill, Oklahoma. I wonder if we are mentioned in their visitor's bureau. "Madill, Oklahoma: Home of the Hit Gay Adult Movie Series *Texas Tales*."

Nah, I doubt it…

We finally made it home late that night. I couldn't wait to take a long, hot shower and crawl into bed and make love to my boyfriend. I walked in the front door, brimming with excitement, relief, and anticipation.

I noticed that it was very quiet.

I went to the bedroom; no Pierce. The bed was made, the house was clean. Too clean. It was a definite "what's wrong with this picture" moment. I suddenly turned around in our bedroom and noticed all of his things were gone!

He had moved out!

I wandered through the house, expecting to find a note. Nothing. The man I loved so much had left me! No note, no explanation, no goodbye.

So much for the man of my dreams…

Now his memory would merely be the stuff of legend, wistful love scenes played over and over in my mind in the weeks, months, and years since he walked out on me. I never talked to him again after that.

If he reads this book, I want him to know that I loved him.

I didn't want to ruin his life by dragging him into the porn business. I thought he saw through Dolph Crawford. I thought he saw *me*. I thought he *loved* me. I still see his pictures in advertisements today.

I hope his life was not destroyed.

You were a good man, Pierce. I loved you with all my heart. I hope your life was not affected by the porn movies. I only regret that we didn't meet at a different time, a time when I was more of the man I would become and you were, too. You will always be in my heart and in my fondest memories.

We got the final movies wrapped and finally finished the contract with Vivid. I got my money. And lots of it. I decided to move and travel for a while. I needed to heal. I needed to think.

I didn't answer my phones. I didn't do anymore appearances. I didn't do anymore interviews. I said goodbye to all of that.

I made my peace with it, once and for all.

About a month later I got a message from Ted's roommate. He wanted to know if I wanted the portfolio of the movies that Trac Productions had produced. Without thinking, I quickly told him, "No, Ted can keep that. That was his achievement. He had his money and now he had made his mark in the adult movie industry. He would be a big director, I was sure of it. But for me, I wanted none of it."

There was silence on the line.

Ted's roommate finally composed himself and said "Dolph, you didn't know? Ted is dead. We tried to contact you when he passed, but your phone was disconnected. He wanted to tell you goodbye and say thanks for your help and support over the years. Dolph, he wanted to tell you he loved you for your sacrifice. He knew that you did it just for him, and how much it cost you."

I couldn't talk.

I was speechless.

I promptly hung up and cried for days. I had lost everything, it seemed. My sacrifice didn't save Ted. All it had bought him, in the end, was a few more months. He was taken too soon.

In the end, like so many people before me and since, the porn industry took everything from me. My dignity. My pride. My self-respect. My friends. My business partner. The man of my dreams.

There was nothing positive about it. Once again, I was alone. Although everyone still wanted to meet Dolph, in many ways it was the most alone I had ever felt. Something inside of me became…numb. I looked in the mirror, and I still saw Dolph Crawford.

The gay porn star.

A piece of my soul died that day.

In many ways, it's *still* dead…

7

Going Legitimate

I kept hearing the words that Father Vincent spoke to me as a boy: "No good will come from the path you've chosen. Homosexuality is a sin against God! You must change your ways and ask God's forgiveness. Ask God to save your soul!"

I was beginning to wonder if there was any truth to his message, after all. Had I chosen the wrong path in my life? Not about being true to myself; I was *very* sure that I was homosexual. That was not in dispute.

It was more about my path in life.

I was twenty-seven years old. I looked back over my twenties and realized it was less of a coming of age story, and more like one more drama after another. Like many of my gay friends during that time, I was burying friends too soon. I was too young to be losing my friends. That wasn't supposed to happen until I was in my seventies.

Now it was happening fifty years too soon…

AIDS was wiping out thousand of gays in the United States. Reagan was president then, but it was his wife who was busy campaigning. Her message? "Say no to drugs." Meanwhile, President Reagan was saying no to drugs, too.

Saying not to drug research for HIV, that is. Saying no to drugs that could possibly save lives, sustain lives, and maybe even manage or cure this horrible disease.

In the beginning, I knew guys that would have a simple cold turn into pneumonia and then go into the hospital and die. No one wanted to touch them. The AIDS patients were quarantined.

I remember when Rock Hudson finally released a statement claiming he had the AIDS virus. He was in Paris. He was quickly asked to leave that hospital. The commercial airlines wouldn't let him fly back to the United States. Rock had to book a private plane to carry his dying body back to the good old US of A.

How's that for star treatment?

It was a tough time for the whole gay community. We watched our friends die. We saw how Washington did nothing. We tried to become informed about the disease and prevention. But in the beginning, there was still conflicting information which made it hard to do either.

People thought you could get it from touching each other, and even from the toilet seat. From kissing or from tears. The rumors spread almost as quickly as the disease and, as a result, the Gay Rights movement suffered a major setback. The Jerry Falwells of the world had a field day with it.

"It was a message from God," they claimed with all the fervor and conviction they could muster. "The homosexual lifestyle is deviant and now they will pay for their promiscuous ways." I don't want to get on a soapbox here. (I will save that 'til the *end* of the book!)

But I don't believe God sends messages.

I believe God speaks loudly.

And God has put homosexuals on this earth to teach compassion and love to the masses. God made homosexuals just like he made heterosexuals. God produced a lot of incredible mysteries in this universe. And God wants all of mankind to love and accept one another. He doesn't want there to be division.

God produced diversity in this world so that we may all be different in our very special way. He didn't clone us…science will do that soon enough. I know, I know, I promised not to preach…we will get to my points of view at the end of the book, I promise.

Put it this way: I just knew that things were changing. I could feel it in the air. I moved out of the gay area of Dallas. I took a break from that whole scene for a while. I didn't date. I didn't give anyone a chance to get close to me. I kept a low profile. I didn't want to be recognized or singled out as a porn star.

More than anything, I just wanted to get a legitimate job and have a quiet life. I was more private now than ever. I was conservative with the money I had made from Trac Productions.

I had a small apartment. Anyone who knew me just months after Ted died would swear they were living next to or selling the paper to or delivering Chinese take-out to a little old man, not some retired porn star.

Finally, I decided it was time for me to go back to college. I desperately wanted to get a higher education. I wanted to finally finish my degree. I needed to start working toward a career.

A *legitimate* career.

One that might not pay as much or seem as "glamorous" as the life I'd led for the past few years, but one that I could be proud of. Finally. One that wouldn't send me chasing after yet another dream, but that would give me a pleasant reality I could brag about to friends without blushing.

I knew that I would need to work while I was going to college. But getting a part-time job just wouldn't support me. I was working out at the gym daily now. It was my only sanctuary. I worked out at a "straight gym." I wore a cap low down over my face and wasn't flashy. I kept a low profile, just in case someone in the gym might have seen my films.

The gym was a place I could go and work out my frustrations. It was the one thing in my life that was pure and right and clean and good. For hours I would sit there on one machine or another, or loping around the treadmill, again and again and again, exercising (*exorcising?*) my demons away. Saying goodbye to old lovers and dead lovers and old friends and dead friends. Every day I left the gym I felt pounds lighter, and it wasn't just water weight.

One day I saw an ad for a massage school.

I called the school and went in to get a massage. I had never had a professional massage before. The school was small, not a lot of flash and dash, but there was something about the people who worked there. They were very kind and gentle. They were relaxed and centered and extremely focused on learning and practicing massage.

I talked with the owner after she finished my massage. I was so relaxed. I thought how good that felt, and how good I would feel passing that feeling on to others. A good feeling that came about of something legitimate, trained, professional and, best of all, without any sexual undertones.

This, I knew, was something that I could learn as a trade. I could get licensed in three months by going full-time, and then start college in the fall. Best of all, I felt that I would be good at massage.

I could make a good living and put myself through college at the same time. On my own terms. Legally. I signed up that very day. I knew it was the first step to getting that legitimate job.

The experience I had while going to massage school was incredible.

The teachers were very knowledgeable. The courses were extremely educational and the practical work was something I really enjoyed. The students would work on each other at the end of every day, so I was getting massage on a daily basis.

Basically, I was studying massage, breathing massage, loving massage, *living* massage. I needed to be there. I felt it. I needed balance. I needed spiritual awakening. It was so different from what I had experienced on the sets of all those movies, or on all those stages dancing as Lance, or in the beds of all those strangers as an escort.

Talk about "going toward the light!"

I read more about meditation and massage and studied the meditation part as closely as I studied the massage part. By the time I graduated, I felt renewed, both personally and professionally.

I felt balanced; I could breathe again.

I truly looked forward to my massage career, and it wasn't too far in the offing. The first job I had in massage was at a very exclusive spa. It was a resort that people would visit for the week or the weekend and get a massage and exercise and relaxation the whole time they were there. It was great.

I worked on about eight clients a day. It was a great way for me to perfect my massage technique. The days were long, and I certainly didn't make as much money as I was used to making, but the work was rewarding and, best of all, legitimate.

I was relieving the stress of others and I was learning more about myself through my own meditation practice. Soon, another milestone would transcend my life: That fall I enrolled at the local community college and officially began my college career.

I was mostly taking required courses, but so was everyone else and although in my late twenties I was not just the "big man on campus" but sometimes felt like the "old man on campus," the experience was as rewarding as my massage career.

I wasn't sure yet what I wanted to get my degree in, but I knew the first two years were mostly required courses, so I would have time to make my decision about a degree later. It felt good to put my life on cruise control and simply enjoy the moment for a change.

For so long I had been searching for myself, reeling from job to job, lover to lover, career to career, always searching for that quiet little boy hiding his sad little secret. Now there were no more secrets, no more lies, and nothing *but* time. Now I knew how Whitney Houston felt in her breakout movie role: For the first time in years, I allowed myself to…. *exhale.*

I started doing massage on my own.

I had a few clients follow me from the spa, and I placed an ad in the local newspaper for new clients. At that time, there were no special sections for licensed massage therapists, as there are today.

Instead, advertising was placed in the same category as "escorts" or "rub downs," so you can imagine the kind of response I was getting. Even though I was clear in my ads about being licensed and being legitimate and draping was required, I still got the sex clients.

I suppose it was inevitable…

No matter how hard I tried to "go legitimate," it was like a mantle I couldn't escape: Dolph Crawford, the Porn Star. See his new role as "Licensed Massage Therapist." Yeah, right.

Wink, wink.

Nudge, nudge.

Still, I did all I could do to stay on the straight and narrow. I moved into a more spacious two-bedroom apartment and set up the second bedroom as a massage studio. I lit candles, dimmed the lights, played Enya, and created a very relaxing space for my clients to enjoy.

As soon as my ad hit the newspapers, my phone was ringing. I was doing massage in the afternoon and the evening and attending classes at the community college in the morning.

Needless to say, I didn't have a social life. But I had finally set some concrete and attainable goals for myself and I was determined to stick with them. I was determined to be legitimate. I was determined to get my college degree.

No matter what…

Meanwhile, my massage business was thriving. Not surprisingly, I would get predominantly male clients. Mostly married men with children. The classic "bisexual" client in search of the taboo.

They would usually come from work in their business suits with their wedding rings on. They would talk about the wife and kids and make it clear to you that they were "straight."

Very, *very* straight.

Then, when I finished massaging them, they would inevitably ask how much I charged for a "release." A release? I would always explain that I was licensed and wasn't going risk my license—or break any laws—just to give somebody a "release." I would inform them that I was a legitimate massage therapist, thank you very much.

Some would get offended. Some would get quiet. Embarrassed. Others would get downright mad. One guy tried to touch my crotch after I told him only three minutes earlier that I was a legitimate massage therapist. These so called "straight guys" were insatiable; they just wouldn't take "no" for an answer.

I remember one client in particular, he was a well-known televangelist. After I finished his massage and rang up his bill, I returned to the massage studio thinking he was dressed. Far from it. Instead, I found this so-called man of God on his knees totally naked with hundreds of dollars spread out on the floor.

He asked if he could worship my dick!

Needless to say, I didn't give him a chance to worship anything but the outside of the front door as I pushed him through it and slammed it in his holy face. Far from being unique, stuff like that happened all the time. I was polite in the beginning, but I soon got pretty hardened to these constant advances.

By now I had been pumping iron for quite some time and I was edging up to nearly 200 pounds of solid muscle. As a result, I took on a tough persona. If you treated me with respect, I would treat you with respect. But if you tried to grab my crotch during a massage, I would throw your ass off my table and ask you to leave.

And I only asked politely once.

After that, I got downright *impolite*…

I had definitely changed from that polite young man from King's Pharmacy back in Bridge City. Remarkably, however, some things from the old town still remained the same: I was definitely a person "on the grow."

In fact, I was now growing into a "no bullshit" kind of guy.

I wasn't going to spare your feelings if you came into my home, into a professional setting I had worked hard to cultivate, and requested a professional massage by a licensed professional.

If you disrespected my profession, I would disrespect you. I would give you one warning if you tried anything during the massage. If you didn't heed my warning, I would stop the session, direct you to get dressed, and inform you the massage was over.

I would add that you had wasted my time.

Therefore, I would not be refunding your money. Not today. Not tomorrow. Not ever. No one dared cross me when I switched from gentle, soothing masseuse to the irate bouncer I could become.

I always remember thinking: "What are these guys willing to risk? They have a wife, kids, a good career and a name in the community, how do they know I am not a cop? Were they willing to risk everything for a stupid hand job? Why didn't they just call an escort? Or, better yet, get one of my porno's and just jerk off to it?"

Well, the answer was obvious: In my experience, the cops didn't go after the clients. In fact, during my brief encounter with escorting not one client was ever arrested. But you can bet your ass several of the *escorts* were.

If you really want to stop prostitution, I believe you should go after the client. They have more to lose. The escort needs the money; he will most likely bond out of jail and be back at work in eight quick hours. The client, on the other hand, will lose the wife, the kids, the job, and not to mention be ostracized by the community as a "sexual predator."

Or will he?

(Huh. I would like to analyze that in my *next* book.)

It's obvious to me that the politicians in this country, many of whom, like my dick-worshipping televangelist, use the services of escorts, both male and female, are merely giving lip service to their so-called "war on prostitution." (Why do you think Heidi Fleiss' "little black book" was never released to the media?)

But I digress.

Once I made it clear to the sexual predator clients that they got nothing but massage, my business soon dropped off. I had *some* clients that only wanted a massage, sure, but that wasn't near enough to pay the bills. The sad thing was, I knew I gave a good massage.

After all, I had been told so many times by *true* massage clients. But I was once again put in a catch twenty-two: If I stayed with just doing massage, I wasn't going to make enough money to get me through college.

But if I did anything sexual during the massage, I would risk losing my massage license. The state law was very clear on that. The major question was: Is it a risk I was willing to take?

The answer, for once, was no!

Around this time I had a friend named Tammy who was also a massage therapist. She had been doing massage for as long as I had. She was a gorgeous blonde with a great body. She had big boobs and looked a little like Pamela Anderson. Not surprisingly, she also had an incredible business.

She advertised in the same place that I did. She was making good money. I told her about my dilemma. "Sweet heart," she said, her sexy voice dripping in that homey Southern drawl, "you have to make the client believe he's going to get what he wants and, in the end, when he doesn't get it, he will come back a few times thinking he *will* get it next time."

That was easy for her to say, most hetero men would lie on her table and stare at her big boobs and then go home and give themselves a manual release just thinking about her.

But my clients were a little more "touchy-feely."

Tammy did hotel calls and even hired other therapists to work for her. That was way too much work for me. I still had school to get through and that was my top priority. I was in my third year by now, so close and yet so far.

By now, I had finally decided to get my degree in education. I really wanted to teach and possibly travel the country and lecture about the homosexual lifestyle and even AIDS awareness. That was still very important to me, and in fact I saw it as kind of a calling. After all the harm I'd done in my life, I looked forward to finally doing some good.

I kept up with all the local gay issues through the local gay newspaper, the *Dallas Voice*. (That is still an excellent newspaper today, by the way.) After Tammy and I spoke about my business, she was determined that she could help me. One day she met me for lunch and we talked about the possibilities of me helping her. And, in return, she could help me.

Tammy knew that I accepted credit cards. I had great credit and had no problem getting a merchant account. I accepted all credit cards, even American Express. At that time, it was hard to get a merchant account with a bank and, worse yet, even harder if they thought you were running a massage business.

I was lucky: My bank president had known me for years and she knew I was a legitimate businessman. She knew that was important to me. Anyway, Tammy needed to be able to accept credit cards from her clients and she couldn't get a merchant account from her bank because of her past credit record.

Now Tammy told me that if I would let her run charges through *my* merchant account, she in turn would give me a percentage of each transaction. It sounded too good to be true. After all, I really needed to spend more time studying. I was now attending The University of North Texas.

I was in the education department, taking all my education classes. The transaction fees from Tammy's accounts alone would mean I could do less massages and still keep up with my bills, which in turn meant more time to study and concentrate on what was really important to me now: Finishing school.

I thought about it overnight and met with Tammy the next day. I immediately told her that I would agree to let her use my merchant account. I told her that she would have to pay the taxes on her transactions, and I would pay her monthly from my merchant account whatever she ran through the account.

Minus my percentage.

She agreed.

"You see, buttercup, things have a way of working out," she said soothingly. "You just concentrate on your education and I will run enough money through your merchant account so that you can supplement your business with the percentage you make off my customers."

Boy, was she ever right.

At the end of the month she had run so much through my merchant account that I was able to pay my taxes and some bills and, as luck would have it, my tuition that semester!

It worked out great.

Each month her balance was higher and higher.

It soon began to double.

I knew she was busy and I knew she had a lot of people who worked for her, but I had no idea she was making *that* kind of money. It was unbelievable. It got me through my junior year at UNT and then onto my senior year. As a result, I was determined to graduate in 1997.

I had been attending college off and on for almost six years. I didn't take many hours at first, because I was busy with my massage business, but as time went on I took more and more college hours as the dream slowly became a reality. I didn't give up. I was ready to graduate. I was ready to do my student teaching and get my education certification.

It was all finally falling into place.

Or was it?

The percentages Tammy was paying me from the use of my merchant account were practically supporting me my senior year. Her business was booming. All I really did was go to school and keep up with her charges and deal with any charge backs. There weren't many.

But there *were* a few.

One time in particular, I remember that the client she charged was a hotel client. He used his credit card for the service and tipped her a large tip. The tip was so big, however, he no longer wanted to pay it.

He eventually told the charge card company that she was doing *more* than massage. And she negotiated the tip for sexual services. When the bank sent me that information, I immediately met with Tammy.

I told her to be honest with me and tell me the truth about what had happened. She told me that the client was drunk and got out of hand. Fortunately for her, he had already tipped her before the massage began. She said he got angry when she refused his sexual advances and she finished the massage and left. She assured me that she did nothing "inappropriate."

"Darling," she soothed in that slow southern drawl, "if I did sex with all of these guys, I would be a millionaire by now. Trust me, they're not getting anything but a good massage."

I believed her.

I knew how clients could be. I had experienced it myself. They get mad and they don't want to pay when they don't get what they want. I didn't think Tammy should have to lose money because some horny client didn't get his "release."

I wrote back to the credit card company and told them that I would *not* be refunding the money for the service. As far as I was concerned, the service had been provided.

It was a legitimate massage and he put the tip down and he signed it. I sent the bank a copy that showed his signature on the card and on the tip and total. It was obviously not a forgery; everything matched up perfectly. The bank credited the money back into my account and charged the customer back for the charge.

And that was that…

I had one semester left before my student teaching began. I had chosen a local middle school where I would be doing my student teaching. I filled out all the paperwork and was accepted into the student teaching program as soon as I completed my senior coursework. It was all finally coming together. I had worked so hard and I was soon going to reach my goal.

I would be graduating after I finished student teaching and then I would apply for teaching jobs and I wanted to tour during the summer on a lecture circuit and speak about gay rights and AIDS awareness. That was the least I could do in memory of Kevin and Ted and all the friends and clients that had lost their lives from this devastating disease.

Dolph Crawford was fading in the rearview mirror.

But, as always, he would soon catch up with me…

8

The Sting

After the overcharge incident, I still had my massage business. I wasn't as busy as Tammy, not by a long shot, but I would still get new clients from my ads. I usually took more bookings over the holidays because I had a break from school for a month. Then I would return and finish my coursework and begin student teaching.

In December of 1996 I got a new booking from my ad. The man on the phone booked the massage in the evening. I greeted him when he arrived, as I greeted all my clients.

I usually invited them in and brought them into my massage room.

I would then ask them if they had areas that needed more work than others, such as a sore lower back or a stiff calve muscle or a tense neck or shoulder region. I would ask them if this was their first massage. I would inquire if they had any injuries.

Finally, I would explain that I was going to step out of the room and let them get undressed, at which point I showed them where to hang their clothes and told them to get on the table, lie face down, and cover themselves with the sheet I had provided. I would knock and enter once they were settled in.

From the very beginning, this client was different. His personality was not what I was used to. He was sort of scraggly looking, as if he might not be able to afford a massage in the first place. He had wild looking eyes and there was just something about his aura that was "off."

From the get go, I didn't feel comfortable with him. So I wasn't that surprised when I entered the room and found him on the table, lying face up, totally naked. I told him that he would need to be draped and directed him to lie on his stomach, face down. He didn't follow my directions.

He started touching himself and telling me he just "wanted some sex." He said that the last guy he went to gave him a blow job. I got pissed off. I told him to get his clothes on and get out. When I returned to the room after storming off, he was looking through my stuff in the massage room.

I immediately asked him to leave and escorted him to the door. He asked for his money back. I told him there would not be a refund. He read my ad, he knew I was legitimate, and he chose to waste my time and disrespect my profession by breaking the rules and asking me to sacrifice myself, my dignity, and my license by crossing the line for his personal gratification.

I opened the door and let him out.

He was pissed!

I didn't care.

Hopefully, he would learn his lesson and not waste anyone else's time again.

About two weeks later he showed up at my door again. It was January of 1997, and I was still on break from school. This time he showed up without an appointment, which pissed me off even more. I opened the door and he acted very passive.

He immediately apologized for what had happened before and he asked if he could come inside and "talk about it." I told him to leave the property; I wasn't interested in any explanation.

As I went to shut the door his whole demeanor changed. His eyes got crazy looking and he yelled something and he pushed the door open and was coming at me! But he wasn't alone: He was followed by four other guys!

They were yelling! Rushing me. Screaming. Shouting orders. I didn't know what the hell was going on! I started fighting these guys! They were trying to get me on the floor face down! I wasn't sure if they were going to kill me or rape me, but I wasn't going to give in without a fight!

We fought for what seemed like an hour, but it was only about 10 minutes in reality. They finally all jumped me at the same time and managed to get me on the floor. One of the guys put his knee across the back of my neck and cut off my airflow. My body went limp.

I thought I was about to be murdered. I thought of my family, my mom, my sister, Dana, I thought of Kevin, and Ted; I felt I would see them soon. I turned my head, gasping for air. When I did, I noticed the back of one the guy's jackets. It read, "Dallas Vice!"

I was shocked and relieved at the same time.

I finally relaxed and the four guys handcuffed me. The scraggly guy told me I was "under arrest." He didn't tell me what for. He didn't even show me a search warrant. But search they did. More officers arrived and went through my apartment, tearing through drawers, knocking over figurines that my grandmother, Effie, had given me when she was still living.

They went through my creatine (a bodybuilding supplement) and even tested it for cocaine. They took my phones, some bank statements, and the very personal and private journals that I had been keeping for years. They sat me down on a chair and took turns questioning me about my "association" with Tammy.

"So *that's* what this is about," I thought…

They wanted to know where she was. They wanted to know why I had all these children's books in my house, since I obviously didn't have children. Some made comments about how the convicts were going to "love me in prison." Others commented on "what a nice clean house I kept" and how I would "have to teach his wife how to clean."

Meanwhile, the other hetero, redneck cops would all laugh at the stupid homophobic comments of the other officers. One guy wanted to know how I could afford to have such nice furniture and expensive clothes if I was a college student. They took all my bank statements, tax returns, they emptied my desks. Eventually, they found pictures of my porn star days and immediately commented how they had themselves a "celebrity cocksucker."

It was a nightmare. I felt trapped, emotionally raped, in my own house. There was nothing I could do. I was handcuffed for the entire humiliating process. I had to sit there and take it. I flashed back to when I was younger and boys at school would call me a "sissy" or a "fag."

It was the same type of boys standing there in my apartment that day, the only difference, really, was that they were wearing a badge and by law they could do whatever they wanted to me.

I was sternly informed of that by one officer when he went to set his dirty ass on my white linen sofa. I asked him not to sit on my linen sofa because it wasn't scotch guarded. He took out his gun and put it to my head and said, "Listen, bitch, I could blow your head off right now and that would be one less fag that AIDS didn't kill."

Shocking enough, but it was the next thing he said that stuck in my head: "You just try to take this case to trial and when the jury sees your fag ass on those sex posters we found and finds out you're a professional cock sucker, they will find you guilty for sure."

I knew then that they were trying to break me.

But despite their bleak cop humor and redneck insults, that remark was probably the truest statement any of them had spoken yet. After hours of going through my apartment, they took me down to the Dallas police station. As soon as we got there and were in public, of course, they got really nice.

They finally put me in a room by myself, where I sat alone for twenty minutes, pondering my uncertain fate at the hands of these homophobe rednecks. Then the door opened and in walked in a guy I thought looked familiar. It was: He was the detective from years ago that had tried to bust me when I worked for Kevin.

"Well, well, well," he said, reveling in the reunion, "we meet again. I told you I would bust your sorry ass, faggot. I see you've been a busy boy, sucking cock on camera. You know, I busted Kevin and I always knew it was just a matter of time before I busted you, too!"

I said nothing in reply, which only infuriated him all the more. I just sat there, thinking Kevin was more of a man than he would ever be. He finally left the room. Other detectives came in with a file. It was pretty thick. They showed me pictures of Tammy. They wanted her.

Bad.

They wanted to know where she was.

I told them I didn't know where she was if she wasn't at her home. They asked me about the merchant account agreement, and I explained to them that I let her use my merchant account because she had poor credit. They told me that one of her girls had gotten busted committing prostitution.

Turns out they had set up a sting on Tammy's operation and followed the path of money to my merchant account. They told me that someone had tipped Tammy off that she was being investigated and she had skipped town.

In her stead, they were charging *me* with promotion of prostitution, the same thing they had gotten Kevin on, since technically I had "profited" from the services of "prostitutes" by allowing Tammy to run her assets through my account and pay me a percentage.

I felt like I was having a waking nightmare.

This was not happening. I had to try to speak, try to save myself. In that dim, stale room, I cleared my throat and told these men that "I had no idea that Tammy was involved in prostitution. Yes, I had let her use my merchant account but I never thought that what she was doing was *illegal*."

The officer that knew me from before spoke up and commented, "Yeah, I know, you thought it was all legitimate just like your homo boyfriend was all legitimate. You are so innocent, and everyone around you is breaking the law. Boy, you are just one naïve faggot!"

I stopped the questioning then and asked to contact my attorney. I knew this didn't look good; my past was finally coming back to haunt me. Only this time, a jury of my so-called "peers" would get to listen to some state prosecutor bring up my past. It wouldn't look good.

Naïve or not, I knew *that* much…

I felt like one of my former adult film models, crying to me that their face was in every adult bookstore in the country and it was ruining their marriage, or their shot at a promotion, or their relationship with their boyfriend.

Only, in this case, I was ruining my shot at *freedom*…

I couldn't put myself in that situation. I would have to consult with an attorney. God help me! I thought hustlers were bad, until I started trying to find an attorney, that is. The criminal attorney is not far from a hustler, in my opinion: They're all full of shit and will do anything for a buck. Preferably, your *last* buck. I finally found a guy that I could afford, got bonded out of jail, and met with him to discuss my case.

Afterward, he met with the detectives and told me that if I would testify against Tammy when they caught her and give them any information that I knew about her and her operation, then I would have my sentence lowered to a misdemeanor and given two years deferred. I would plead "not guilty" and, as long as I didn't break any laws in the next year, would be released with no finding of guilt.

The only other option I had was to take it to court. If the jury found me guilty, and we both believed that they would, I would be looking at a felony offense, which would ruin my chances for ever having a legitimate career.

In the back of my mind, I kept remembering what that cop had said about the jury and how they would look at my past and find me guilty. As stupid as he might have been, he was dead on target with that comment. I couldn't take that chance. I had to plead not guilty and take probation.

I was not a criminal. I knew I could make it through probation: I didn't drink or do drugs, and I could pass a mental observation no problem. I thought that probation would be the best for me.

As a result, I pled "not guilty" in front of Judge Warder. She was very respectful, which came as a relief after my harsh treatment at the hands of the cops. I somehow sensed that she thought this was a stupid case, but I still couldn't chance taking it to trial. I wasn't that confident about my attorney, either.

He was a joke, let's just leave it at that.

So now, at a time when my life should have been about change and reaching my goals and helping the kids of the world cope with their sexuality and keep from getting AIDS, which had by now become a national epidemic, it was about criminal courts and probation and testing.

Oh yes, testing.

I was honest about my homosexuality, which surprised the probation department because most people kept that a secret. But in the good ole state of Texas, they still think homosexuality is "deviant sexual behavior."

They even sent me to a doctor that tests sex offenders, sexual deviants, and pedophiles. They questioned me many times in counseling as to why I wanted to teach children and, more importantly, to them anyway, *what* I wanted to teach children. Was I going to try to convert children into being a "homo like me?"

It was like I had stepped into a time machine and gone back to the Dark Ages. I kept expecting to be shut into an Iron Maiden or put on the rack or have holes drilled into my skull to "let the fag out."

It was scary, not for me, particularly, but because these folks really believed this bullshit. I had to comply with the testing or they would revoke my probation. It was that simple.

So I met with a doctor that gives a plethysmograph test.

This is an actual, honest to goodness test that, get this, "measures sexual deviants." In other words, it tests to see if you're gay or a pedophile. (I learned that, in Texas anyway, these two terms are literally interchangeable.)

The way the plethysmograph test works is that they put you in a room by yourself. There you sit in a recliner and they place an electrode on your dick to test your level of sexual arousal—or lack thereof—while you listen to tapes of adults trying to have sex with kids or gay males trying to have sex with each other. And then they put in what I call the "hetero tape," which contains sounds of a man seducing a woman.

The doctor interviewed me prior to testing. He asked me questions about my homosexuality. I was honest with him, as I have been with you. He told me that most guys lie about being gay, but his test "always measures accurately that they are truly homosexual or a pedophile."

He was sure that I would test homosexual in the "top 80 percentile." Yes, they actually have "percentiles" for this kind of thing, based on his interview. Well, I went in there, sat in that stupid recliner, let them attach an electrode to my penis, listened to the disgusting tapes and, when I was finished, he told me to meet him in his office. When I walked in he was in the process of printing out my test and, furthermore, he did *not* seem pleased.

He pointed to the area of the test that showed whether or not I was attracted to children. According to my results, to no one's surprise but his own, apparently, there was zero attraction to children. I wasn't surprised by that, neither was he, it turned out. But then he showed the homosexual test.

When listening to the homosexual tape, I had no reaction. Then he showed me the hetero test result. While listening to the heterosexual tapes, I measured 98% arousal! I started to laugh. He did not find it very humorous. He accused me of "lying about my sexuality."

To that accusation, I only laughed louder.

"You've got to be kidding me," I replied, adding wryly, "I have spent my whole life being true to who I am. I have lost friends and isolated myself from my family, all because I was gay…and now you're suggesting that I have been lying about being gay and that I am really *straight*? I find that about as stupid as I find your test."

I thought for a moment, surrounded by beakers and vials and tubes and computers and spreadsheets, and then asked him, "Have you ever thought that your computer *can't* measure human sexual arousal perfectly? If you've never pondered that, then maybe you should now. I have spent my life lying about being gay, not about being straight. The bottom line, doctor," I concluded, "is that your test doesn't work."

Then I got my coat and I left.

I was so outraged at having to be put through all that. I thought about the person who may have tested arousal to the gay tape or the pedophile tape and truly wasn't either. I marveled at how this stupid test could have ruined that person's life forever.

I just couldn't understand that science could be that black and white. I wasn't a psychologist, but I knew that human sexuality was not black and white. Being gay didn't mean I was attracted to *all* men, just like being heterosexual didn't mean all men were attracted to all women.

Attraction, unlike science, was all about the subtle nuances that drew us to each other. Men to women. Women to women. Men to men. Women to women. A scent. A joke. A certain height, or shade of eye, or depth of voice.

An expensive watch…

And it wasn't just one thing, it turns out, but many things.

Pierce hadn't been my type, not at all, but still I fell harder for him than I ever had anyone in my life. That was what attraction was all about, not some electrode strapped to your dick!

I finally got through probation. Judge Warder released me after a year with no finding of guilt. I was just finishing my coursework at UNT. Amazingly, I had continued with my studies through the whole probation fiasco. I was determined not to let anything stop me.

Then the day finally came for me to start my student teaching. Student teaching would take twelve weeks and then I would graduate with my degree in Education and take my state board test for my teaching certificate. I was focused. Pure and simple. I was ready to put my past behind me and go forward into a legitimate job.

But the State of Texas wasn't quite through with me yet...

The day before I was supposed to begin student teaching I got a phone call from the middle school's administrative office. It seemed that someone had tipped the school off that I had been arrested and charged with a "sexual crime."

It was an issue of "moral turpitude," they said and, although I was released with no finding of guilt, I would not be able to do my student teaching and, furthermore, I would not be able to graduate from UNT.

I couldn't talk; I was literally speechless. It was like the spine had been sucked straight out of me and my body was jelly. I fell to the floor and screamed, "Why!? Why?! Why me, God!? I did everything right. I have paid my debt to society. I proved my innocence!"

I couldn't go back to being a hooker, to dancing, to hustling, to porn. I just couldn't. I'd been shown the mountaintop, I'd climbed all that way and seen what "straight life," could be like, and now I couldn't go back. I just couldn't! I wanted a shot at a normal life! I cried myself to sleep that night...I just didn't know where to turn or what to do.

EPILOGUE:
One American Boy

You know that saying about "a good night's sleep?" I'm not a big believer in things like that, but in this case it really was true. The next morning I woke up. The sun was shining, the birds were singing, and spring was beginning.

A changing season…a new day.

I pulled myself out of bed and I thought about my Dad who had taught me, in his own rough fashion, to be tough. I remembered back when I was thirteen-years-old. I came home from school one day and went out to the garage to find my brother's weights.

As I was looking for the dumbbells, my Dad came home. He immediately wanted to know what I was doing "rummaging through the garage."

I said, "Oh nothing."

He seemed to sense that something was wrong.

He walked up to me, turned me around, and saw my face. I had been beaten up. For a split-second, I saw compassion flicker in his eyes. Then he turned back into a typical Texas Dad and asked me what had happened. I told him a guy at school was picking on me; he had said that I threw the football "like a girl."

Then I started to cry.

My Dad sat there quietly for a minute and asked me how the fight ended. I told him that I ran away from the bully. My Dad then sat me down and looked me right in my bruised eyes and said: "Son, you never start a fight with anyone; but if someone challenges you, you never run away! You always stand and finish the fight—and you let the bully know that he better think twice before he challenges you again."

My Dad was right.

My whole life, I always ran and let the "bully" win. I always sat quietly and took the abuse from the homophobes in my path. But that was then; this was now. I was now 5' 10" and 225 pounds of muscle, courage, and strength. What was I afraid of? I was no longer a little boy.

Finally, at long last, I was a man!

I picked up the phone and called the Dean of the University. I told him that I had taken the courses and paid the tuition and passed all the tests. I added that I was on the dean's list at UNT.

I wanted my diploma.

I *demanded* to be able to graduate. I told him if he wanted a fight, he would get a fight. I told him that I had been kicked around and beaten up by others like him and I was not going to run from this fight.

Not now, not ever.

I would get what I was owed!

Two weeks later, I received a letter from the Dean of Students. She advised me of my rights, and explained that she had scheduled a hearing with administrators, faculty, and students of my peers.

There was that word again: "my peers."

Well, I seriously doubted if seven gay men or women would be sitting on that board, but I could only hope that whoever *would* be sitting in judgment of me would at least be fair.

The dean told me to bring "character witnesses." They would have a chance to speak and then I would have *my* chance to address the board. She warned me that the school had grounds to deny me my diploma, but nonetheless I would have my chance to speak.

That's all I wanted, finally, my chance to speak!

They say in Texas they do things bigger. Well, I'm from Texas, dammit, so I didn't just bring a character witness or two, I *filled* that room with character witnesses. My sister, Dana. John, my friend who was a school administrator. My professors who had taught me at UNT.

My clients wrote letters. Some of them were very well-known in Dallas, and they believed in me. It amazed me how many people come through for me. I was so blessed. And even with all those heavy hitters I believe that it was my sister, Dana, who made the most impact.

As I told you earlier, Dana was the shy one in the family. She was nervous about speaking in front of a group of people. I was so proud of her. This was a tough room. When it was her turn to address the board, I was astonished. She stood up and looked at everyone and then she paused.

I held my breath.

Then she began to speak, and I couldn't believe her strength.

"Members of the school board," she said, her voice clear and strong as tears welled up in my eyes. "I have traveled hours to stand before you today. But I would travel across the world for this man.

"He is my brother. But most importantly, he is my friend, and he is the most loving, caring, compassionate man that I have ever known. He is a great uncle to his nieces and nephews. A loving son to my parents, and a gentle brother to my sister, my brother, and I. He has stood by me in my darkest hours.

"He held my hand when my husband walked out on me after fourteen years. He lifted me up and encouraged me when I thought my life was over. He helped me get a job and get out of a dead end town.

"Today, I am an independent woman, making my own living, having my own life. Independent from any man. I like myself more than ever before. I am able to stand before you today because of this man—my brother. He would be a wonderful teacher…because he has taught *me* so much.

"If you deny him his diploma, then you deny the youth of tomorrow a great education. I cannot express in words what my brother has taught me about life and love and people and survival. I can only imagine, if given the opportunity, that his potential is endless.

"In closing, I would like to say that I don't believe that the University of North Texas is *giving* my brother anything. He has earned it. He put in the hours of studying. He took the tests and he worked hard and paid his tuition. If you deny him what he has worked for, then you and your university, in my opinion, are thieves."

The room was quiet. No one spoke. Out of all the other distinguished, articulate guests that I brought with me to the hearing that day, it was my sister Dana's speech that moved me the most. It obviously moved the board as well, because everyone was stone silent.

It was almost as if they were pondering every word my sister spoke. Then it was my turn. I had made copies of all my letters from distinguished character witnesses. I also put a copy of the lie detector test administered by the State of Texas, showing that I was not lying about not being involved in promotion of prostitution.

I began addressing the board.

I simply asked: "Has anyone in this room ever made a mistake in life? If you haven't, raise your hand." No hands were raised. I went on. "I admit I have made some bad choices in my life. But if I hadn't made bad choices and learned from my mistakes, I might not be standing before you today. I now have sixteen years of cumulative education. Four of those years in higher learning. But, most importantly, I have thirty-six years of *life* experience.

"I have been on top, successful, well-known, and financially secure. I have been on the bottom: broke, scared, beat up by police, and put in jail. Even worse,

I had to go through the Texas probation system. I am a living example of an American success. I was placed in a world where 'my peers' were not like me, but I learned to cope. I learned to respect their rules and ways of life.

"I have dealt with loss; I have buried more people than I care to count. I have endured more heartache than most men my age. But I have prevailed. I complied with your curriculum. I took your tests and I mastered your program. I paid you in full for tuition. And now you dare to judge my moral state!

"We live in a country that separates laws and rules from morals and religion. Whose morals are we following at this university? Who dictates what is decent and what is not? Everyone has a choice in how they live their life. Men and women have died so that we can have a choice about how we choose to live our lives and make our own decisions.

"When I paid my hard earned money to your institution, you never questioned my morals. Nor did you ask where the money came from. I don't care how you view me or my morals. I have been judge by heterosexual people all my life! But before you judge me as a man, know my story. Until each and every one of you on this board can do that…then you cannot begin to judge me!

"In closing, I would like to believe my 'peers,' this board, will find it in your hearts to do the right thing and give me the diploma that I have earned. I hope that the State of Texas will allow me to take the State board test. I know I will be a great teacher, because I have been a good student in school…and in life!"

After I finished, the dean made a brief speech and read some bylaws and then the board was adjourned. We waited for one hour as the board decided my fate. I was so moved by my friends and my sister showing up to support me…it really meant a lot. The board returned with its findings: "The University must in good faith allow me to graduate and grant me my degree in education."

I would not, however, be able to complete my student teaching and apply for my teaching certificate. They would not take the liability of having me around young children because of what they called "the nature of my record."

The board adjourned.

My "peers," it seemed, had chosen to cover the University's ass. The University of North Texas was not going to support me. To this day, I still get alumni letters from UNT asking me for money. I tear them up with pride and in return do NOT support the University.

I got my diploma in the mail. I call it my $12,000.00 "piece of artwork." After all, I can't do much with it but hang it on the wall. When I go to professional offices now and I see all their diplomas and certificates proudly displayed, I often wonder…wouldn't it be better to have documents to show what we have *really* achieved in our lives?

From November 19, 1999 until today April 18, 2004 I have been gagged by the State of Texas. The state will not allow me to speak, write, or draw pictures of the last four years of my life. If I do, I will go to prison for a very long time.

This is under the orders of a conservative Texas judge. I have taken these last four years and pondered my path and life. I have spent many hours meditating and listening for messages that lie within me.

I have finally gotten the message.

I understand I clearly now. You see, I have lived my last forty years based on fear and shame. I was ashamed of being different, so I kept it a secret. Eventually, people found out my secret and tried to use it against me. I feared being alone. I feared that I would never find love again. I feared life. I withdrew from society because I feared I couldn't cope.

I was afraid of the pain.

I watched television and saw our world change on September 11th. I saw Americans grow closer. I have seen more gay movies and sit-coms establish themselves into mainstream popular culture. I have seen celebrities publicly "come out" about their sexual identity and, far from spurning them, I saw the public *embrace* them.

I have watched as public opinion changed into acceptance of gays and the gay movement. I am finally growing proud of the modern American heterosexual. They are, it seems, accepting our olive branch. They are showing compassion and understanding, thanks in part to education, enlightenment, and most of all the support of the media and the press.

I am so proud of this country and proud to live in America. I didn't waste the last four years of my life. I spent them meditating and listening and breathing. I finally discovered the answer. The answer is: "Live in truth, not fear." That may seem so simple, but it is so powerful.

The *truth* is so powerful…

If you do wrong, own it, tell the truth. Don't put a gag order on someone because you have powerful attorneys and can manipulate the law. Simply live in truth. Don't gag someone else's truth! If you declare war on a country, don't feed it to the American people or Congress that it is to remove a dictator…don't insult our intelligence…tell the truth!

Explain to the American people that we as a country have grown dependent on Saudi Oil and since it was Saudis that hijacked our planes and killed thousands of people on our land, we must develop Iraq as our new oil reserve and get that flowing and then deal with Saudi Arabia and Osama.

Tell the truth!

If you are afraid of change in this great country and you want to go back to the 1950s, then I suggest you leave this country and move to the Middle East, where radical fundamentalists will be glad to have you join their religious agenda. Don't try to change the constitution to fit your religious right agenda.

Don't fear change. Fear censorship! Howard Stern is NOT the monster! If you really listen to him he is pro-gay, pro-choice, and trying to evoke people to wake up and take this country back!

I know he is shocking sometimes, but shocking brings him ratings and that brings him advertisers and it works in this free market system.

I have a newsflash for you: John Ashcroft is the *real* monster, folks. He is all about censorship. In my opinion, the Bush administration may be trying to defeat the Taliban, but yet they are becoming the same religious fanatics in the process.

Let's not live in fear, let's live in truth.

That's how I plan to live the rest of my journey on this earth. I plan to speak the truth as I travel this great nation and address large auditoriums of people filled with gays, straights, and bisexuals.

How, you may ask? Well, I plan to speak the truth as I write my next book, **Secrets and Lies:** *The Dirty Sheets.* I plan to speak the truth to you, my friends, always. And I ask that you do the same.

I hope you have learned from my journey. I hope that you never have to endure the same path. I hope that you now know you are not alone in your suffering. I hope to pave the way for the future. The last word from Dolph Crawford has not been spoken—or written.

May truth always prevail…

APPENDIX

Homosexuality 101

I wanted to add a section in my book that answers some common myths about homosexuality, AIDS, and the so-called "Gay Agenda." It is my belief that the epicenter of homophobia is not hatred, fear, or outrage, but *ignorance*. I hope this section educates the heterosexual community at large and, hopefully, brings about more acceptance—and less hate.

My experience with being able to write about gay issues and bring my view to the following pages is not that I have a Ph.D. in Human Sexuality. It is because I was born homosexual.

I have been homosexual for forty years in the Bible belt of the south. I made my living in the sex industry, escorting, adult films, and massage therapy. I include massage, not because it was a job in the sex industry, it wasn't, but because it enabled me to learn so much more about the bi-sexual male or the married, "closeted" male.

Little did they know it, but my massage clients were in a one-on-one therapy session for about an hour with me. They usually confided in me, much like they might in a session with a formally trained psychologist. So, while giving massage, I also learned a lot about the plight of the "closeted" male.

I have also volunteered many hours of my time answering the phones at the local AIDS resource center. Much of that time was spent answering questions about "safe sex" and AIDS awareness. I also have my own personal view, aside from the CDC (Center for Disease Control) based solely on what I have observed in the last twenty-three years of the AIDS crisis.

So that's my resume, kids. When I speak, I speak from MY experience. I don't speak for homosexuals as a group. I speak for MYSELF and about my personal experiences as a homosexual male.

From what I have seen so far in the media, there really isn't a gay spokesperson, formally speaking. I hope that this section will answer some questions for you, enlighten you, and possibly even educate you.

After all, that *is* what I got my degree from the University of North Texas in: Education. It is only through education that we begin to learn and open dialogue about issues that, until today, were veiled in secrecy and considered taboo.

I hope this extra chapter lifts that veil, and shines the light on TRUTH.

Common Statement:

"Homosexuality is a choice."

I have heard this misnomer quoted often throughout my forty years on this earth. It is usually quoted by religious groups who are trying to promote their agenda and prove that being gay is a learned behavior or, in their opinion, a so-called "devious behavior."

This couldn't be further from the truth. I was born homosexual. Being homosexual is my biological orientation. I have been aware of my attraction to men as early as eight years old.

Now, here is where it gets into a gray area; there is a range of sexuality.

Some men are 100% homosexual, others are 50% homosexual, which gets into the bi-sexual area. Still, most are 100% heterosexual. Each individual falls somewhere along that spectrum. (Keep in mind I am staying very basic here, scientifically speaking, because I don't want to lose the average reader by quoting some scientific theory.)

The main problem, in my opinion, is societal pressure. If you are socialized to believe that homosexuality is "sick, wrong, perverted, and a sin against God," then you are most likely going to hide or mask your sexual identity.

Some men, I have found, can spend a lifetime hiding it, get married to a woman, have children, and sneak around in parks, adult bookstores, and rest areas to find temporary sexual gratification with a male. That man is usually conflicted, but retreats to the safety of his "safe" hetero-life in the suburbs, where his secret is safely hidden.

Unfortunately, I have witnessed this to be a disaster in the long-term. In my opinion, the woman in that relationship is greatly damaged. She didn't get a totally equal partner; she got someone who she thought was always there, but was often not, either emotionally and/or physically. She deserved a 100% heterosexual male. In the end, as happens so often, she eventually begins to think that something is wrong with *her*.

One of my massage clients was a perfect example of this: He was a successful businessman from Houston. He had three children and a wife and a high-profile social standing in the community. His wife raised his children, but she eventually became dependent on alcohol and prescription drugs to try and fill the void in her marriage.

Meanwhile, he was promiscuous in rest areas, bookstores, and parks before moving on to male escorts. He contracted AIDS and committed suicide in their country home, far away from his perfect River Oaks mansion. When he died, his secret died with him.

The obituary simply read: "Wonderful father and loving husband."

What is the Answer?

Remove the shame.

Write books, like this one, make more documentaries, open up communications. Educate young people. Show homosexuals in a positive light. We've seen enough of the stereotypical feminine homosexual. Not all homosexual men identify with that. Instead, why not show masculine, all-American homosexuals?

Good looking, smart, articulate, successful, powerful, and strong homosexual men. Only then will the true masses start to tune in. People have to be able to relate to the character. We must remove the stereotype of the feminine, witty gay male, not entirely, but certainly as the "only" gay male that we ever see on TV or in the movies.

We must represent all gays and lesbians as a diverse and wonderful group of people. I will do my part when my book is released to represent myself and my community in the best possible light.

I hope that the media and the press will allow me to do just that and give me the same high-profile exposure that they give some sports figure or Dr Laura. I will make myself available to travel the country and speak to the masses and hopefully evoke change in this great nation.

As always, change takes place one person at a time.

Only by changing *our* world can we change *the* world…

"What Should I do if I Feel my Son or Daughter is Homosexual?"

This has been asked of me on several occasions. My answer is always the same: You love your homosexual child the same as you love your heterosexual child. You make sure that the child feels safe and has an open line of communication with *both* parents. You don't use the words "sissy," "fag," or "queer" when describing homosexuals. You create a safe haven for you child to develop in.

Don't push the child to "come out" and admit he is homosexual. In my opinion, this whole idea of "outing people" is wrong. Let that child reveal himself to you and his peers in his or her own time.

If the child isn't interested in sports, don't push it. Don't force it. Find out what he *is* interested in and develop that. I was horrible at sports. Remember: I threw the ball like a girl.

But I loved working out.

I started working out with weights and developed my body and felt a great sense of achievement in that. Let your child find his own niche, whatever that may be. Give him time.

Don't treat him as if he was "special" or otherwise single him out. A child doesn't want to be singled out for being "different." My guess is that if you are a loving parent, you are already his best friend.

When he is ready to tell someone, he will naturally tell his best friend first. Don't worry about special schools. Remember, he will have to cope in the real world one day. He must be able to socialize with heterosexuals, good and bad. If he has a strong support system in his family, he will ultimately prevail.

I remember watching *The View* one morning on ABC. As usual, the hosts were sitting around the table discussing their lives. As I recall, Meredith Vierra was discussing her son getting a haircut.

Apparently, it was a very short, in her words, "gay haircut." When her son came home from school he was upset and told Meredith that it was because the kids at school were making fun of him and suggesting he had a "gay haircut," so he must be gay.

I was so impressed my Meredith Vierra; what a healthy relationship she had with her son in the first place because he immediately confided the school incident with her. But what she did next moved me: She explained to her son that there was nothing wrong with being homosexual and that if that's what kids thought about him at his school, then those kids were not his friends.

In her own simple way, Meredith was breaking a stereotype with her kid. I am sure her first instinct was to protect him. But she took it one step further and completely shot down any stereotype.

You see, if kids don't think it is a big deal, they automatically let it go. Meredith didn't make a big deal out of it. She simply redirected those emotions back onto the kids that were making the accusation in the first place. But she left her child feeling as if the incident was "no big deal."

I was so moved by that, I wrote her an Email, in which I thanked her for being a very good Mom. I am sure she will raise some very healthy children, psychologically speaking.

The Idea that Homosexuals are Pedophiles or Try to "Recruit" Young People to Become Homosexuals:

This I can speak to from personal experience. When I was arrested by the Dallas Vice in 1997, they couldn't get anything on me. I admitted I was gay from the beginning. Therefore, when they saw I had a lot of children's books in my home then, in their minds, I must also therefore have a "fascination with children."

They didn't want to hear that I was a student getting my degree in education. No, they needed an "angle" to bring to prosecutors so their case would be "stronger." Remember, they were raised in the south by some heterosexual parents that equated gays with child molesters.

This couldn't be any further from the truth. As part of my probation, the state ordered that I receive what they called "sex offender counseling." I dutifully attended and found that it was mostly convicted pedophiles.

The therapist realized I didn't belong there but, in the few meetings I attended, I observed a cross-section of men that were convicted and trying to be rehabilitated for "indecency with a child."

The therapist explained to me that there were a "very small percentage of pedophiles" and that they were "mostly classified as heterosexual." The men who came through his office were considered what are known as "situational sex offenders."

This means that they were around young people and sex presented itself and they were aroused and there was inappropriate touching, etc. In other words, it wasn't premeditated.

The therapist said that most of these men, given the chance, would have chosen an adult sexual partner over a juvenile. But with a true pedophile, the predator will reject a room full of adult partners and seek out a child. Pedophiles are a very small percentage in society.

But they are still dangerous, in my opinion.

If you talk with children who have been abused sexually by an adult, it's usually a relative or a stepfather, etc. "Situational sex." I found that to be very interesting. So why do homosexuals get accused of being child molesters? To me, the answer is quite simple: Because it is that religious agenda of hate again.

If you can make a parent believe that the homosexual will molest a child, then a parent will hate the homosexual. It's a proven way to get people to follow your agenda…an agenda of hate and ignorance.

It's happening right now with the Internet. That's the "new devil." The government wants to control the Internet. Well, how do they convince voters to let them do that? They publish articles on child pornography on the Internet. Once again, they push the easy button by evoking fear in parents and convincing them that the Internet needs to be regulated.

Think for yourself, folks!

Don't live in fear!

Live in truth!

And as for the idea of recruiting children into the homosexual lifestyle? I am living proof that you can't be "recruited" into any lifestyle. I was raised in the Bible belt surrounded by a population of KKK members.

Everything in my life was heterosexual.

I had it socialized into me from day one that a man and a woman were supposed to marry, have kids, and live "happily ever after." In my opinion, it started with Walt Disney's animated children's movies and books.

Well, folks, Dr Laura, and Jerry Falwell, you couldn't recruit me. I sought out homosexuals who were like me, whether it was in a gay bar or a rest area. I wanted to be with "my culture."

The culture that I was born to exist in.

This is not to say I couldn't co-exist in either culture; I *can* do that. I have many friends and family who are heterosexual. But their recruitment didn't work on me. Neither will it work on a homosexual recruiting heterosexuals. This is a myth. This is a religious agenda. This does not happen.

So, parents, rest assured: Your kids are safe. We are not currently accepting new recruits. We only want to pave the way for understanding and compassion so that if your son or daughter *is* gay, they will not have as tough a time in society as we did.

If a Person Experiments as a Teenager with Same Sex Activity, Does That Make Them Gay?

No. Experimentation is similar to what we discussed earlier. It's "situational sex." You become a teenager and suddenly your hormones are racing. You might experiment with someone from the opposite sex or with someone from the same sex. You are simply experimenting.

It's not written in stone that you are homosexual because you mess around with your buddy from school. It's simply experimentation. Now, I know that most parents don't want to think of their children experimenting with other teenagers, but folks—it happens. And if you're truly honest with yourself, it probably happened when *you* were a teenager and no one ever talked about. It was kept quiet and you and your friend never discussed it the next day.

If ever…

I believe that is very normal and justified and expected. It's all about discovery at that age. It's about coming into your own. And understanding who you are and where you fit in. Now, keep in mind that when I mention "experimentation," I am not talking about penetration. I am simply talking about touching and fondling and experiencing someone else's body.

In my case, it happened when I was about fifteen. It started with neighborhood friends, mostly boys. But then I *did* have experiences with girls, too. I enjoyed both. But I was much more attracted and sought out the boys. Or they sought me out. I wasn't as interested in returning to the experience with girls.

The real problem with becoming homophobic usually surfaces around this age. Let's say you're a young boy and you have situational sex with another boy. You may have enjoyed the experience, but you're not homosexual.

You have guilt about the experience because you have been socialized to believe it's "wrong." You then turn that guilt into self hate and then you act out in hurting or possible killing a gay male.

Possibly, in your mind, that is symbolic in killing what you may fear inside of you. Do you see how crazy this can get? We know it happens; we see it in the press all the time: Gay man found dead, beaten to death, hung on a fence, left to die, pick one—or all—of the above.

People always seem so shocked when this happens. But I always think about the murderers and why they could do something like that. My guess is it starts with experimentation. As I said before, I am not a psychiatrist. These are only my personal observations. I would like to see a psychiatrist do research on my theory and let's see if I am right.

But remember, kids: If you are experimenting, you are simply encountering someone else's body out of curiosity. It doesn't make you homosexual. You know in your heart if you're homosexual.

Just be true to who you are.

As for the trend right now for young girls to run around and make out with other girls like Madonna and Britney did? That's just for shock value. It doesn't mean they are homosexual or bi-sexual; they are just emulating their pop culture idols.

I don't think Madonna or Britney were trying to "corrupt" young people like the FCC would like you to believe. They are artists and they were expressing their art. They knew it would create a news story and that's free publicity.

Remember Roxie Starr's line from Chicago: "And that's Showbiz…Kids!"

Is Using the Word "Queer" of "Fag" Unacceptable?

Yes. In my opinion, both words being used are in bad taste and should be removed from shows like Queer as Folk and Queer Eye for the Straight Guy. The word "queer" means "strange" and is disparaging when describing a homosexual.

I am not strange.

Using these words commercially, somehow, makes it acceptable to put that idea out in mainstream society. I am glad both shows are successful and I support them. But I think we should eliminate using the word.

Much like we did with the "N-word."

I know some black people still use the N-word when referring to someone within their race. In the gay culture, some gays use the word "queer." But in society we should cease to use those words because they have a negative connotation when describing a group of people.

If we are going to show acceptance and solidarity and respect in mainstream society, we must eliminate such word as the "N-word," "fag," or "queer." It's negative and it's not productive. (Besides, the word "fag" is French for cigarette and I don't smoke.)

Once again, my focus is to eliminate the prejudice in society so that young people who discover they are gay are not made to feel "less than" or "bad" about who they are. That is why I make these pleas as a forty-year-old adult: I am secure now with who I am and have been called worse by many homophobes.

I believe that if these prejudices wouldn't have existed when I was a teenager first discovering my sexuality, then perhaps my life would have turned out better. Maybe I would have been a healthier adult sooner. Perhaps I wouldn't have experience self-hate and chosen some of the paths that I chose.

Paths that were destructive and painful.

Just a thought…

What is the "Gay Agenda?"

You hear this term a lot. Usually it's describing the gay culture in a negative light. In my opinion, the only agenda I—or any other tax-paying gay citizen—have is to acquire the same rights as any other American citizen. Legal marriage. Not civil union. The ability to legally adopt. Change the sodomy laws.

"Gay agenda" simply means give the homosexual man or woman the same rights as any other tax-paying American citizen. Simple. No, not with the current Bush administration, which is pandering to the religious right. It is outrageous that Bush is threatening to change the Constitution of the United States.

That, to me, is so typical of a little rich kid who is used to getting his way. If he doesn't win, he changes the rules. We don't need someone like that in power. America is the greatest country in the world. We are the example to the rest of the world as to how democracy works.

In four years, Bush has given the oil companies what they wanted: Iraq. And now he wants to give the religious right what they want, which is nothing short of an end to any equal rights for homosexuals.

I recently watched the HBO series, *Ironed Jawed Angels*, which was about the woman's movement. It was so shocking to me that there was a time when women were second class citizens.

They couldn't vote, hold property, or accept jobs of equal pay. These women were true heroes; they risked everything for what the constitution already promised: "Equal Rights and the Pursuit of Happiness." But it is no different from today with the homosexual movement.

I didn't take my case to court because I knew that in Texas if my sexual orientation was brought out in court I would not win. I have been in a relationship where my partner and I built a life, including a house and finances. Everything was combined. However, the house was in his name.

When we split, I didn't have any law to protect me. I had to take what he *chose* to give me. If we would have been married, I would have had the law to protect me and split the marital assets down the middle.

Who does it hurt if homosexuals are given equal rights? Well, let's see. Who did it hurt when women were given equal rights? Who did it hurt when the blacks were given equal rights? It hurt the white heterosexual male. He didn't want the competition.

Now he has to share a water fountain and a job with women and blacks. He does not want to share these things with the homosexual, too. It's too much competition for the homophobic, misogynistic, racists, white hetero-male.

But here's the good news: The white heterosexual male is *not* the majority. The rest of us have to vote and get politicians that hear our voice. Plain and simple. *That* is the Homosexual Agenda.

What is Safe Sex?

How do I Protect Myself from AIDS?

The only way to protect yourself from any STD is abstinence. But most people don't choose that method. So let's break it down for the rest of us: If you are having sex, you have to use a condom. If you use a condom, don't use petroleum based lubricant as it will tear that condom.

HIV is transmitted through blood and semen. If you are having anal sex or vaginal sex, then there could be tearing. Most males that I have known who have contracted the HIV virus were "bottoms." (I know that this is not scientific, but bear with me. This is the voice of experience talking here.)

The CDC still considers oral sex to be a high risk for contracting HIV. I disagree. Because if you have an open, bleeding sore in your mouth you are not going to want or desire to give oral to anyone. I have known men who were very promiscuous and are still living today…mostly because they were not a bottom, which means they did not let anyone penetrate them anally.

There are many other diseases out there that you have to be cautious of. Syphilis is back and the cases are at the highest levels than ever before. Use condoms. Don't use drugs or alcohol to the point where you don't know what you are doing and you don't have safe sex.

Be responsible. Protect your body. I don't care what your mate says. If he doesn't want to use a condom, then he doesn't respect you or your body. Love yourself enough to protect your health. Get tested and be safe. I want you around for a long time. We have a lot to do, you and I.

What are My Plans for the Future?

I get this question a lot. Personally speaking, I am still single. I am self-employed. I am still fighting legal cases. But I would have always remained a private person if November 19, 1999 would have not happened.

I decided to write this book because the universe kept pushing me in that direction. The fiasco that happened to me in Dallas. The blatant abuse of justice that I saw. Remember forty years ago when President John F. Kennedy was killed in this city, and it was all covered up?

Well, trust me, not much has changed. But sometimes you have to hit rock bottom before you assess what is going on around you and begin to make a comeback. I believe that my plans for the future are to be a voice.

In my small way, I want to devote my time and my spirit to helping the cause of the homosexual movement. I will speak and be open for interviews. I will give my opinion based on my experience. I will always tell the truth. I will write other books. I hope to leave my legacy for change.

I hope that when I am no longer on this earth, my books will still be read. My voice will still be heard. And, most of all, I will motivate you to use your life for change and truth and justice for all men and woman, gays, and straights, Jews and gentiles, rich and poor, black and white.

May God Bless You and May God Bless This World...

About the Author

Dolph Crawford, a humble boy from a small town in Texas, went on to become one of the porn industry's most prolific actors, producers, and eventually…directors. In that capacity he produced movies through his own production company, Trac Productions, for the porn powerhouse, Vivid Video.

Dolph's movies, so popular they are now anthologized in some of Vivid's best-selling "best of" series, including: *4 x 4*, the *Texas Tales Series*: *Volumes One, Two, and Three, Three the Hard Way, Men-TV*, and *Hard to Hold*, to name just a few.

Dolph holds an Associates and a Bachelor's degree from The University of Texas. Dolph was also licensed in sports therapy for 15 years in the state of Texas.

Contact Me:

You can contact me for personal appearances, readings, and book signings at

DolphCrawford@aol.com

0-595-32079-1

www.ingramcontent.com/pod-product-compliance
Lightning Source LLC
Chambersburg PA
CBHW061306280526
45784CB00002B/912